Fabulous Chain Mail Jewelry

Creating with Components

Marilyn Gardiner

Kalmbach
Media

Kalmbach Books
A division of Kalmbach Media
21027 Crossroads Circle
Waukesha, Wisconsin 53186
www.JewelryAndBeadingStore.com

Published in 2018
22 21 20 19 18   1 2 3 4 5

Manufactured in China

ISBN: 978-1-62700-448-0
EISBN: 978-1-62700-449-7

Editor: Erica Barse
Book Design: Lisa Bergman
Photographer: William Zuback

Library of Congress Control Number: 2017934276

Contents

Projects

Appendix of Weaves

Introduction

What's in the book?

This book is all about using chain mail weaves to make components, and then use them to build fine jewelry. The projects are directed at women who like to make beautiful accessories to complete the outfits they wear for work and play.

You'll find projects that use chain mail components to:

- link metal connectors
- link beads
- build dangles
- build bails and beads
- build shapes
- showcase jewelry artists

APPENDIX OF WEAVES In addition to expanding on my theme of components, I've also separated the instructions to make a project from the steps to learn a weave. The Appendix of Weaves section includes new weaves that weren't in my previous book, as well as new, improved ways of constructing old favorites. (For example, I've used plastic canvas as a tool for starting three different weaves.)

I hope the Weaves section will encourage you to keep this book (and my first one) at hand as a reference as you work on all your future projects. The step-by-step photos are designed to facilitate independent learners who work at their own speed. I've also created a Plan of Action for each project. It's an overview of the strategy you'll use to complete the piece of jewelry.

About me

I'm a retired teacher, revitalized as a jewelry designer and teacher of chain mail classes. I'm a Canadian based in Waterloo, close to Toronto, Ontario, and I have taught classes across Canada. My husband, Brad, makes our jump rings, assembles my kits, and transports everything to shows. We winter in Tucson Ariz., and I teach at shows and stores there, in Texas, in Milwaukee Wis., and in Buffalo, N.Y. When I get dressed in the morning, I need to put on clothing and jewelry. Both need to work together and make me feel good—prepared to meet my day—whether it be for work or pleasure, at home or away.

My guiding beliefs

I have some strong beliefs about making jewelry—or for doing most tasks in daily life. There's seldom only one right way to do anything. The goal is to accomplish the end result as carefully and efficiently as possible, given one's current skills, knowledge, and physical ability. Listen to good advice, but then experiment to find your best way to do the task at hand. While the end goal is quality work, the process should be enjoyable. Think of the cliché about "stopping to smell the roses." You're not running a race, after all.

When you learn something new, ask yourself, "What if..."

What if I want to add a row on each side of this chain using a different weave?
What if I wanted to make earrings to go with this?
What if I want to use this necklace idea but try it in a different weave?

I believe this is the secret to developing your creativity. You won't be surprised to hear each project ends with a section called "Explore and Experiment." I encourage you to explore the possibilities for each project. Ask yourself questions: How could I make this more casual or more elegant? What could I change to make this fit my lifestyle? YOU get to play and then decide.

Tools & Materials

Tools

Let me tell you about some new tools I've added to my tool collection since the last book. Yes, I could be labelled a tool junkie, but only a small number of the ones I try out make it to my everyday tool case (flatnose, chainnose, cutters, and roundnose) **A, B**.

Pliers

Tronex came out with a new pair of flatnose pliers that have a short, stubby, flat nose (#747). I like to use them in my right (dominant) hand when I'm opening/closing rings. The design adds significant leverage, especially for the thicker gauges of wire—they're a dream to use **C**.

Xuron has a line of chain mail pliers that I like for lighter gauges of wire, and for working in tight spaces. The ones I use the most are the short, flatnose (#483). There is a new, chisel nose (#487) that a lot of maillers love, and bentnose is a possibility, too. Another pair are called tweezer nose pliers (#450), which are helpful for micromaille projects **D**.

Plastic canvas

My biggest discovery this year was found in the needlecraft section of my local craft store. It's called plastic canvas, and will be instantly recognizable to anyone who does needlepoint, a form of counted thread embroidery. The kind I use comes as an inexpensive package of several 4-in. (10cm) plastic squares that can be cut to smaller pieces with scissors. This canvas is described by the number of holes per linear inch. The one I use is "7 count"—it has seven holes per inch. You can also buy 5, 10, and 14 count.

Why do I consider it so useful? In the past, I've used masking tape or pieces of wire to stabilize the start of several weaves. I've even tried punching holes in an old, plastic, loyalty card. Both these methods work, but they're painful to use in comparison to the plastic canvas **E, F**.

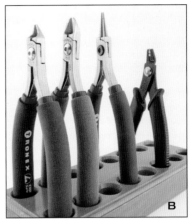

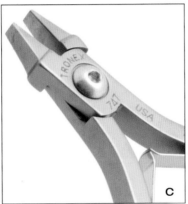

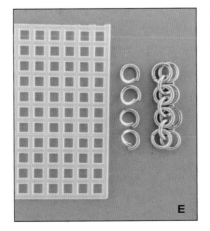

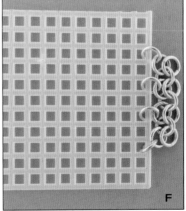

Materials

Jump rings

Should I buy them or make them? Buying rings is a good way to start out. It ensures well-made rings with smooth cut ends that will fit together perfectly, and be the correct size and gauge for the weave you want to make. It also means that you don't have to invest in equipment and wire until you decide that you need to be able to custom make your rings.

What metal should I choose?

Do you prefer silver, bronze, copper, gold-filled, rose gold, or colors available in anodized aluminum or niobium, or enamelled copper? Start with the ring sizes and gauges specified if you want successful results. You can't just substitute rings you have on hand.

Wire gauge

The most common method to measure the thickness of wire is a gauge system. There is the American Wire Gauge system (AWG) and the British Standard Wire Gauge System (SWG). The AWG system is typically used for precious metals and the SWG for ferrous metals. There are reference charts available that specify in millimeters or inches the thickness of wire in either measurement system.

In this book, all the wire gauges used are AWG. In both systems, the lower the number, the thicker the wire—so 14-gauge wire is very thick, and 20-gauge wire is much thinner.

Ring sizes

To make a jump ring, you wind wire around a metal rod to make a coil. Then it's cut with a saw along the length of the coil—and the jump rings fall off. What's important in chain mail is the diameter of the rod that was used to make the rings. If a rod that measures 4mm across was used, then the inside diameter (I.D.) of the resulting jump rings is 4mm.

Imperial vs. metric

Here's another quirk. Some rods are measured in fractions of an inch, and others are measured in full, half, or quarter millimeters. Not knowing the gauge system of your rings could inadvertently cause confusion or error as you purchase supplies or make a project.

If you are unable to find rings in the gauge system of the instructions you are following, you can do the math and change from one gauge system to another. You can also learn about Aspect Ratio (the relationship between a rings diameter and wire gauge) and deliberately choose to use a heavier or lighter wire (and the resulting different ring sizes) than called for in the project.

Aspect ratio (A.R.)

How can you use different sizes or gauges of rings with the same chain mail pattern?

I start with what I know. I know that 18-gauge 3.5mm I.D. jump rings make a nice, compact, Byzantine weave. However, I want to make a heavier chain with 16-gauge rings.

Before I can do any calculations, I need to have the wire diameter (W.D.) and the inside diameter

(I.D.) of the rings both in the same measurement system. So, I find the W.D. for 18-gauge (1.024mm) and 16-gauge (1.291mm).

The first calculation is to find out the aspect ratio (A.R.) of the ring size I know works well for Byzantine.
A.R. = I.D./W.D.
A.R. = 3.5/1.024
A.R. = 3.42

Now I want to find the I.D. for a 16-gauge ring. Cross-multiply, and
I.D. = A.R. x W.D.
I.D. = 3.42 x 1.291
I.D. = 4.42mm

This tells me a 4.5mm I.D. ring should work. Next, I might want to find a ring size to use for a more delicate, 20-gauge Byzantine chain. I find the W.D. for 20-gauge wire is .8128mm.
I.D. = A.R. x W.D.
I.D. = 3.42 x .8128
I.D. = 2.78mm

That tells me to try 20-gauge 2.75mm I.D. jump rings (and yes, it makes a lovely chain!). For more aspect ratio information, visit https://marilyngardiner.com/make-jewellery/student-resources/ to download a pdf tutorial.

Basic Techniques

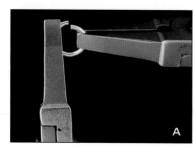

A

Opening a jump ring

Use two pairs of pliers to hold the sides of a jump ring with the opening at the top (12 o'clock). (I prefer flatnose pliers because they provide more leverage, are easier on my wrist, and are less likely to mark the metal.) The pliers in your left hand hold the side of the ring steady, while the pliers in your right hand turn that side of the ring toward you. (Reverse if you are left-handed.)

Closing a jump ring

Use two pairs of pliers to hold the sides of a jump ring with the opening at the top (12 o'clock).

Bring the ring ends back together by rotating the wrist of your dominant hand and exerting a bit of inward pressure. You will hear a "click" as the ends touch. The goal

is for the two ends to line up exactly with no space between them.

Move the ends back and forth by small amounts to adjust the fit. If you go a bit past where they are even, they will spring back and match exactly. Spend the time to close each ring carefully—this is the mark of a professional finish **A**.

Making loops

Many of the projects in this collection use wire-wrapped loops to add components—there are simple loops, double loops, and wrapped loops. Sometimes loops are made on a headpin that holds a small bead, several beads, or a pendant bead. In other cases the loops are at both ends of a length of wire that holds a small bead, several beads, or a pendant.

I like **simple loops** because you can open and close them just like a jump ring, so they are easy to add to your work. But there are some things to consider: If the wire is "soft" (like craft wire). If the gauge is very fine, be careful. If the loop will be at risk of being pulled apart, then choose a different wrap. If the bead is just going to dangle, then it will be fine. If the wire is "hard," then a simple loop can be a good choice (see the "Sweet Chrysocolla Necklace," p. 33).

Double loops are easy to make and are quite secure. See "Beau's Bead Necklace," p. 70.

Wrapped loops are the most secure, but they take more practice to perfect—the goal is to make wraps that are even and tight—with the loop centered like a lollipop.

Simple loops

Slide a small closed ring on one jaw of the roundnose pliers, and make a mark just above it with a fine-tip permanent marker **B**. This marks the loop the size you want. You can make additional marks for a larger or smaller loop sizes (wipe off the marks with rubbing alcohol when you're done).

Cut a piece of wire about 3½ in. (8.9cm). Make sure both ends are cut or filed straight across. Hold the very tip of the wire at the mark on your pliers. Run the tip of a finger along the tops of the jaws—you shouldn't feel the top end of the wire **C**.

Use your thumb to brace the wire as you turn your wrist away from you, wrapping the wire around the plier. Stop when the top tip curls around and touches the stem. The loop will look like a "P" shape **D**.

Insert chainnose or roundnose pliers into the loop, brace with your thumb, and give a quick, small twist away from you **E**.

The result is a centered loop. Adjust with pliers as needed **F**.

String bead(s). Bend the wire at a 90-degree angle right above the top bead **G**.

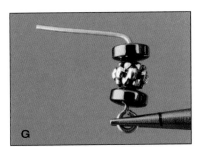

When the end of the wire meets the bend, the loop is complete **H**.

Adjust the loop with pliers if needed. Your goal is two centered loops the same size **I**. If the loops are not both facing the same way, use two pairs of flanose or chain-nose pliers, each one holding a loop, and rotate the loops as needed.

How do I chose a loop?

Consider the amount of space used by the loops. Sometimes you may want the beads to sit close to the connecting chain, and other times the space is fine—it's a design decision. Compare the appearance of the wraps on the pendant in the "Smoky Bronze Links Necklace," p. 16 and on the pendant in "Beau's Bead Necklace," p. 70.

HOW MUCH WIRE WILL I NEED? The best and easiest way to decide the length of wire you will need is to make a test piece. Use inexpensive, soft craft wire of the same gauge you plan to use in your finished piece. Check to make sure that the loop you create is large enough to hold the ring or rings in the actual project: sometimes the link connects to only one ring, but other times there could be two rings. Use a fine-tip permanent marker to mark the sweet spot on your roundnose pliers. You want the size of every loop to be the same. Last, unwind the loops, straighten the wire, and measure the length of your wire piece. As a very general guideline, you'll use about ½ in. (1.3cm) to make a simple loop, 1 in. (2.5cm) for a double loop, and 1½ in. (3.8cm) for a wrapped loop.

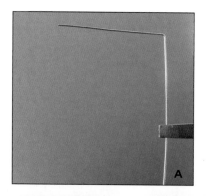

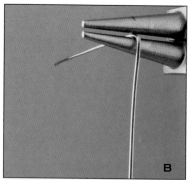

Wrapped loops

Cut a 3-in. (7.6cm) piece of wire and use chainnose pliers to make a sharp bend about 1¼ in. (3.2cm) from the end **A**.

tip Look for a 6-in. (15cm) metal ruler that has metric as well as inch markings—one where the measurements start right at the edge. This will let you measure the wire and cut off a length right against the end of the ruler. You can also use the end of the ruler to make a sharp 90-degree bend in the wire.

With roundnose pliers, grasp the short side of the wire right at the bend, lined up with the mark on the pliers. Hold the pliers perpendicular to the work surface. The wire end will point away from you **B**.

Grasp the short end of the wire end with your fingers, lift it up and around the top jaw, and then pull downward until it's pointing to the floor **C**.

Pull the pliers out of the loop. Place the lower jaw of the pliers back into the loop at the same spot on the pliers' jaws **D**.

Grasp the wire end with your fingers, and swing it under the lower jaw and up until it points away from you **E**.

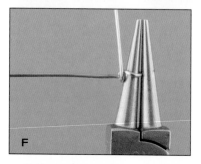

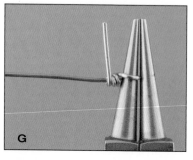

Point the pliers to the ceiling. Swing the wire around the stem to make the first wrap **F**. (At this point you could remove the loop from the roundnose pliers and instead hold the loop with chainnose pliers while you complete the wraps.) Continue to wrap the wire around the stem. Make about three wraps **G**.

Remove the loop from your pliers. Use wire cutters to cut off the excess wire. Use chainnose pliers (or crimping pliers) to carefully press the tip of the wire against the stem **H**.

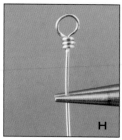

String a bead(s) on the wire. Press the tip of your chainnose pliers against the end bead, and make a sharp bend in the wire. (This creates a bit of space for the wire wraps and allows space to insert your round-nose pliers.) With roundnose pliers, grab the bend of the wire at the mark on the pliers **I**.

Create another wrapped loop as in photos **C–H** on the other side of the bead **J**.

Double loops

Use craft wire to make your first double loop. Then, unwind the loops and straighten them so you can measure to see how much wire you will need to make a loop of the size you want. In this example, I used a 2-in. (5cm) 22-gauge copper headpin to wrap three beads **A**.

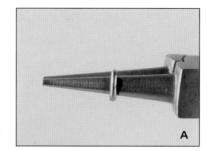
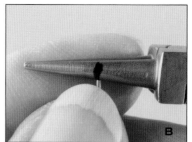

Hold the wire vertically in your non-dominant hand; and hold the pliers horizontally. Place the top of the wire between the jaws of the pliers, right at the mark, so the tip of the wire is almost hidden and you can't feel the top of it with your fingertip **B**.

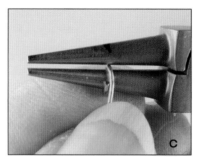
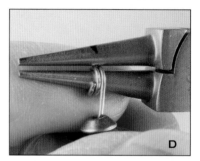

Use the thumb and fingers of the hand that is managing the wire to keep the wire pressed against the bottom jaw of the pliers as you rotate the pliers away from you **C**.

Your wrist will only rotate so far, so release the tension on the pliers while you rotate the pliers back to the starting position. Then tighten the pliers up on the wire, and rotate them away from you again. Keep repeating this process while the wire wraps around the bottom jaw of the pliers. Continue to press against the wire as you work in order to get a nice, snug, round loop **D**.

After the first complete loop, guide the wire so it sits beside the previous loop (like a coil), and continue looping the wire until you have two complete loops **E**.

Notice that you have three loops—but you only want two. Next, very carefully cut off the extra loop with flush cutters **F**. (It's all too easy to cut the wrong loop or cut too deeply—be careful.)

The final step is to make a centered loop. Grasp the loop with your roundnose or chainnose pliers—right next to the stem of the main wire. Flick your wrist quickly away from you. This movement creates a bend in the wire stem and the loop will look like a lollipop **G**.

Butterfly Wings Neck Chain

In my search for interesting links, I came across these filigree butterfly wings. The next challenge was deciding on a chain mail weave to create a similar and complementary shape. European 4-in-1 to the rescue! I made a triangle and then gathered up the last row of rings with a larger one.

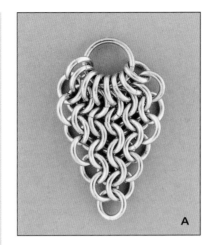

A

SKILL LEVEL: Beginner Plus

WEAVE: European 4-in-1

DIMENSIONS: 22 in. (56cm) necklace with a 2-in. (5cm) pendant

MATERIALS
JUMP RINGS
- **324** 16-gauge (AWG) 4.5mm I.D. (medium)
- **9** 16-gauge (AWG) 9mm I.D. (large)
- **24** 16-gauge (AWG) 3.25mm I.D. (small)
- **6** 18-gauge (AWG) 3mm I.D. (for the clasp)

FINDINGS
- **4** 40x22mm filigree butterfly wings, satin Hamilton gold (BeadFX)
- **1** round toggle clasp, brass (Star's Clasps)

TOOLS
- **2** pairs of pliers suitable for chain mail (flatnose, chainnose, bentnose)

Supplies note: The jump rings for this project were made from round jeweler's bronze wire. These ring sizes also work for Argentium sterling, 10% silver-filled, or copper jump rings. Choose your focal bead first, and then choose the accent beads that pull the colors from the "main event" bead (or ones that contrast with and enhance that bead).

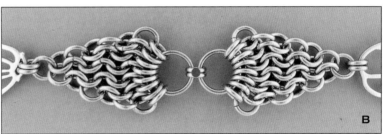

B

Make the European 4-in-1 components and pendant

The necklace is built with pairs of flat mesh components that alternate with the butterfly wing findings. Each component uses 36 medium jump rings and one large ring. Follow the "European 4-in-1" weave instructions, "Build a butterfly wing," p. 98, until you have eight rows. There are eight jump rings in the final row. Open a large ring, gather up the eight rings in the last row, and close the ring. Repeat this step to make eight flat mesh components. The photo shows a completed component; each one is about 1⅝ in. (4.1cm) long.

Now, make the pendant. It is just a bit larger than the ones you've

made, so follow "The repeat" until you have 10 jump rings in the final row. Then gather up those 10 rings on another large ring **A**.

Join the components

Set out two flat mesh components and two small rings. Use the two rings to join the large ring of one component to the large ring of the other (red dot). Repeat to make three more pairs of flat mesh components (for a total of four pairs) **B**.

Build the side chains

Set out one Butterfly Wing link, two component pairs, and four small jump rings. Connect the wing with two rings on each side in between the two component pairs (red dots) **C**. Repeat to make the other side chain.

C

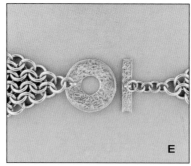

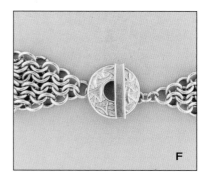

Build the pendant

Set out two wings, the flat mesh pendant, and four small rings. Connect the large ring of the pendant to each of the wings with two rings (see main project photo).

Connect the side chains to the wings

Set out the two side chains, four small rings, and the wings with the pendant. Arrange the pieces so the tips of all of the wings point in the same direction. Make sure the wings are oriented right side up (not upside down). Use two rings on each side to connect the side chains to the wings (red dots) **D**.

Attach the clasp

At the end of one side chain, use a 16-gauge 3mm clasp ring to add the ring part of the toggle **E**. At the end of the other side chain, add four jump rings in a mini-chain. Use a fifth ring to add the loop on the toggle bar **F**.

Make adjustments

The necklace could be made 3¼ in. (8.3cm) longer by adding a Butterfly Wing at the end of each side chain. It could be made quite long by also adding additional flat mesh component pairs. A component pair measures 3½ in. (8.9cm). Adding a wing and component pair to each side would add 10¼ in. (26cm) to the necklace.

 This flat mesh weave can be used in so many different ways: see the bail in "Trizantine Necklace," p. 50, and the rectangular components in "Beneath the Sea Necklace," p. 83.

Explore & experiment

For earrings, you could add a the large ring of a single flat mesh component to an earring finding. European 4-in-1 was used to make armor, and is currently used to fashion garments. It is flexible like fabric and can be shaped in many ways. If this concept is of interest, do some research and make notes about the possibilities. Then start playing and experimenting.

Lusty Links Neck Chain

This is a big, bold, and beautiful chain mail creation. I made it to pair with another silver necklace (see "Chrysanthemum Links Necklace," p. 20). I love wearing these together, especially with a tailored blouse—or any time I want a long, statement necklace.

Plan of action

Make the side chains

. . . .

Add the hammered links

. . . .

Add the chain inside each link

. . . .

Attach the clasp

. . . .

Make adjustments

. . . .

Explore & experiment

SKILL LEVEL: Beginner

WEAVE: 4-in-2

DIMENSIONS: 34 in. (86cm) necklace

MATERIALS
JUMP RINGS
- **8** 12-gauge (AWG) 10mm I.D. (large)
- **42** 16-gauge (AWG) 7.5mm I.D. (medium)
- **177** 16-gauge (AWG) 5mm I.D. (small)

FINDINGS
- **9** 33mm round, hammered diameter sterling silver links
- **1** sterling silver spring ring clasp

TOOLS
- **2** pairs of pliers suitable for chain mail (flatnose, chainnose, bentnose)

Note: The jump rings for this project were made from round Argentium sterling silver wire. These ring sizes also work for 10% silver-filled, jeweler's bronze, or copper jump rings. Choose your links first. If the diameter is different, you may need to adjust the size or number of ring that are inside each link. The clasp is optional if you make the chain long enough to slip over your head.

Make the side chains

Follow the "4-In-2" weave instructions, p. 100, and use the small 16-gauge 5mm rings to make two chains, each with 33 pairs of rings **A**.

Prepare the links

Open four medium rings. Hold a ring in your pliers, add a link, and close the ring. Add three more rings to that link. Repeat, adding four medium rings to each link **B**.

Connect the links and the side chains

Open two medium rings. Hold one ring in your pliers, add on the pair of small rings at one end of a side chain, add on two of the medium rings floating on the end link, and close the ring. Double up that ring

(red dot). Open a large ring. Hold it in your pliers, and add two floating rings from the previous link and two floating rings from a new link (green dot). Repeat this step until all nine links are connected. The end link has two floating rings. Use two more medium rings to connect these rings to one end of the other side chain **C**.

Add the chain inside each link

Open five small rings. These will be used to make a mini-chain that crosses from one side of a link to the other side. Add one small ring to the pair of medium rings at one side of the link. One by one, connect the next three small rings to the first one. The last ring will also connect to the pair of medium

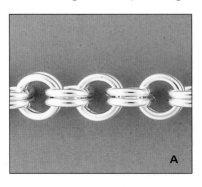

A

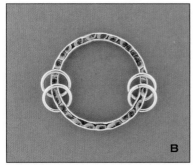

B

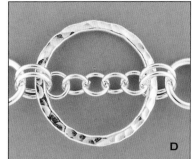

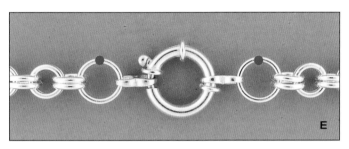

rings on the other side of the link. When you add the final ring, be sure the mini-chain is not twisted. Repeat this step to make a mini-chain across all eight remaining links **D**.

Attach the clasp

Open two medium rings. Use one ring to join the pair of small rings at the end of the chain to a figure-eight loop on the clasp. Repeat with the other ring, the other end of the chain, and the other figure-eight loop on the clasp (red dots) **E**.

Make adjustments

The necklace can be made longer or shorter by adjusting the length of the side chains, or by adding/removing the hammered links.

Explore & experiment

● Have fun playing with different diameters, shapes, and materials when creating your links. If the links are significantly smaller, then the gauge and diameter of the rings should be proportionally smaller, too. This necklace design is very adaptable and uncomplicated to make. I've made this necklace with hollow, rectangular, mother-of-pearl shell beads in a gray color (sold by the strand) for a funky look.

● A dramatic pair of earrings could feature a large link with the inside chain running from top to bottom of the link.

Smoky Bronze Links Necklace

Notice the art glass flower bead by Susan Stortini—that was my starting point. Smoky Quartz craft wire blended with the dark glass color, while a purple Charoite stone bead and mauve crystal pearls rounded out the main materials. Next, I played with different chains, but decided that pairs of the classic Byzantine, along with hammered, oval links, was a perfect combination. A beaded tassel added to the pendant was the final touch.

SKILL LEVEL: Beginner

WEAVE: Byzantine

DIMENSIONS: 36 in. (.9m) necklace with a 2¾ (7cm) pendant

MATERIALS
JUMP RINGS
- **555** 18-gauge (AWG) 3.5mm I.D. (for Byzantine components)
- **76** 18-gauge (AWG) 5.5mm I.D. (for connectors)
- **55** 18-gauge (AWG) 2.5mm I.D. (for the tassel)

WIRE
- 9 in. (23cm) 20-gauge wire

BEADS
- **1** 34x38mm glass pendant bead (Susan Stortini, Toronto, ON)
- **2** 4mm round crystal beads, mauve (Swarovski)
- **1** 12mm round stone bead, charoite
- **2** 6º seed beads, topaz

- **6** 6mm crystal pearls, mauve (Swarovski)

FINDINGS
- **7** 18x12.5mm metal link oval rings, black (TierraCast)
- **7** 2-in. (5cm) headpins, black (TierraCast)
- **1** 15mm lobster clasp, black

TOOLS
- **2** pairs of pliers suitable for chain mail (flatnose, chainnose, bentnose)
- Pair of roundnose pliers
- Pair of flush cutters

Note: The jump rings and wire for this project were made from round, Parawire Smokey Quartz copper wire with a non-tarnish coating. These ring sizes also work for Argentium sterling, 10% silver-filled, jeweler's bronze, or copper jump rings. Choose your pendant bead first, and then choose the large bead below it to repeat a color from the pendant bead.

Plan of action
- Make the Byzantine segments
- Connect the Byzantine segments into pairs
- Link the Byzantine pairs into sets
- Add the oval links
- Wire-wrap the pendant bead, stone bead, and pearls
- Add the tassel to the stone bead
- Connect the pendant to the chain
- Attach the clasp
- Make adjustments
- Explore & experiment

Make the Byzantine components
Follow the "Byzantine" weave instructions, p. 91, to make 36 individual Byzantine segments, each with 14 rings. Use the 18-gauge 3.5mm jump rings **A**.

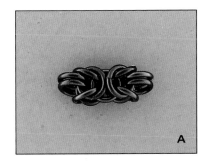

A

Connect the Byzantine segments into pairs
Set out two Byzantine segments side by side. Open four 5.5mm jump rings. Hold an open ring in your pliers, add the end pairs of rings of the two segments. Close the ring. Add another large ring beside it. Repeat to add two more rings at the other end of these two segments. Repeat this step to make a total of 18 linked pairs of Byzantine segments **B**.

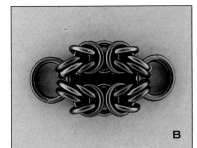

B

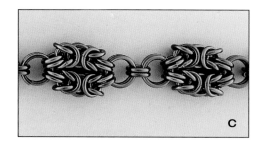

C

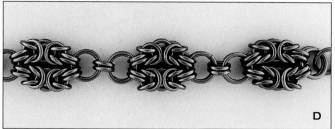

D

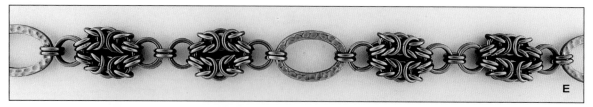

E

F

G

Link the Byzantine pairs into sets

Set out two pairs of Byzantine segments. Open two 3.5mm jump rings. Hold an open ring in your pliers, and add the end pairs of rings of the two components. Close the ring. Add another 3.5mm ring beside it **C**.

Repeat this step to make a total of six sets, each with two Byzantine-pair components.

Set out three pairs of Byzantine segments. Open four 3.5mm rings. Use the above method to link the three pairs end-to-end. Repeat this step to make a total of two sets, each with three Byzantine-pair components **D**.

Add the oval links

Set out the oval links, the Byzantine components, and the

3.5mm rings. Use two rings to connect a two-pair component to an oval link. Use two rings to connect the other end of that component to another oval link. Continue to connect the components and links. Your chain will start and end with an oval link. Finally, add a three-pair component to the oval link at each end of your chain **E**.

Wire-wrap the pendant bead, stone bead, and pearls

To estimate the length of wire needed, measure the beads to be wrapped and add about 1–1½ (2.5–3.8cm). Wire-wrap the pendant bead with wrapped loops (see "Wrapped loops," p. 8): String a crystal bead on each side of the pendant bead **F**. Wire-wrap the stone bead with a seed bead on each side: Make a wrapped loop at the top, and a simple loop at

bottom (see "Simple loops," p. 7). String a crystal pearl on a headpin, and make a wrapped loop. Repeat with all seven pearls (see project photo).

Add the tassel to the stone bead

Set out the pearls, the 2.5mm jump rings, and a 5.5mm jump ring. Make seven chains (one ring into one ring) using 2.5mm rings: three rings, five rings, seven rings, nine rings, 11 rings, and 13 rings in length. Open seven 2.5mm rings. Use the rings to add a wrapped pearl to the end of each chain **G**.

Open the 5.5mm ring, gather up the end ring of each chain, the loop at one end of the wrapped stone bead, and close the ring **H**.

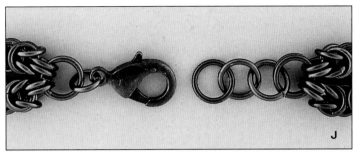

Connect the pendant to the chain

Open three 2.5mm rings. Use one ring to link the stone bead to the base of the pendant bead. Use two rings to link the pendant bead to the oval link in the middle of the necklace chain **I**.

Attach the clasp

Open a 3.5mm ring and three 5.5mm rings. Use the 3.5mm ring to connect the loop on the lobster clasp to the pair of rings at one end of the necklace chain. Connect the three large rings, one by one, to the other end of the necklace chain. This makes a short extender chain for the clasp **J**.

Make adjustments

The necklace can be made longer by adding links and/or Byzantine component pairs, making each side of the chain identical. Of course, the necklace can be made shorter by adding fewer Byzantine component pairs and fewer oval links.

Explore & experiment

● For a simple bracelet, make a single chain of two-pair Byzantine components and add a clasp. Or, place the Byzantine segments closer together by using one pair of 5.5mm rings to pick up the ends of four segments at a time (so only one pair of rings separates each set of two Byzantine pairs)

● For earrings, add a single Byzantine pair to an earring finding, and then finish it off with a drop bead.

Chrysanthemum Links Necklace

The Chrysanthemum component is so appealing that I wanted to use it in a necklace, not just a bracelet. I decided to alternate the components with hammered metal links that were about the same diameter—and I love the result. For comfort, I added simple side chains to sit at the back of the neck. This chain can be worn by itself, or layered with the "Lusty Links Neck Chain," p. 13, for a real impact.

SKILL LEVEL: Beginner Plus

WEAVE: Chrysanthemum

DIMENSIONS: 28½ in. (72.4cm)
necklace

MATERIALS
JUMP RINGS
- **16** 18-gauge (AWG) 6mm I.D.
- **174** 18-gauge (AWG) 5mm I.D.
- **128** 18-gauge (AWG) 3mm I.D.
- **76** 18-gauge (AWG) 2.75mm I.D.

FINDINGS
- **9** 26mm diameter, hammered

sterling silver circle links (Nina
Designs)
- **1** sterling silver toggle clasp

TOOLS
- **2** pairs of pliers suitable for chain
  mail (flatnose, chainnose, bentnose)

*Notes: The jump rings for this project
were made from round, half-hard
Argentium sterling silver wire. These
ring sizes also work for 10% silver-filled,
jeweler's bronze, or copper. The
hammered links are also available in
bronze from Nina Designs.*

Plan of action

Make the
Chrysanthemum
components

· · · · · · · · · · · · · · · ·

Build the center chain

· · · · · · · · · · · · · · · ·

Add the side chains

· · · · · · · · · · · · · · · ·

Attach the clasp

· · · · · · · · · · · · · · · ·

Explore &experiment

Make the Chrysanthemum components

Each Chrysanthemum compo-
nent uses two 6mm jump rings, 16
5mm jump rings, and 16 3mm jump
rings. Follow the "Chrysanthemum"
weave instructions, p. 97, to make
eight components in total. Each
segment is about 1 in. (2.5cm) in
diameter. The photo shows a
completed Chrysanthemum
weave component in copper **A**.

Build the center chain

Open two 2.75mm jump rings for
each Chrysanthemum compo-
nent. Add a 2.75 mm ring through
any two outer rings of a Chrysanthemum, and close it. Add another
2.75mm ring directly opposite the
first one (also through two of the
outer rings) (red dots) **B**. Repeat
this step with all of the Chrysanthemum components.

Open two 5mm rings for each
Chrysanthemum component. Set
out the circle links. Add a 5mm ring
(green dots) through a circle link
and then through a 2.75mm ring
(red dots) on a Chrysanthemum
component **C**. Add a 5mm ring
through another circle link and

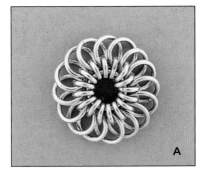

then through the other 2.75mm
ring on the same Chrysanthemum
component **D**. Continue to build
the chain, alternating Chrysanthe-
mums and circle links. This center
section will be 18 in. (46cm) long.

21

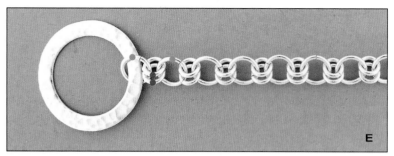

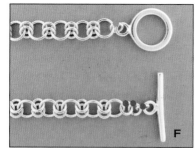

Add the side chains

Each side chain measures 4¾ in. (12.1cm) long. Open a stash of 5mm rings. Close a stash of 2.75mm rings. Each side chain uses 15 5mm rings and 14 pairs of 2.75mm rings. Add an open 5mm ring to an end circle link (green dot) and two 2.75mm rings (red dots), and close the ring. Add an open 5mm ring through the end pair of 2.75 rings, add two more 2.75mm rings, and close the ring. Repeat until you have added 14 pairs of small rings. End with a final 5mm ring **E**.

Repeat to build the other side chain at the other end of the center chain.

Attach the clasp

Open four 2.75mm rings to attach the clasp. Each side chain ends in a 5mm ring. Insert an open 2.75mm ring (green dot) through an end 5mm ring, add the ring half of the toggle clasp, and close the ring.

At the end of the other side chain, add a 2.75mm ring, and close it. Add a second one, and close it. Add a third one, add on the bar part of the toggle clasp, and close that

ring (red dots) **F**. The clasp adds 1 in. (2.5cm) to the chain.

Make adjustments

The necklace can be made longer by adding to the length of the side chains. Or, it can be made shorter by reducing the length of the side chains. Each inch of side chain requires three 5mm rings and three pairs of 2.75mm rings. Remember to add or subtract equally from both side chains.

Explore & experiment

● Use the same three sizes of rings to make more components. Link them together using 3mm rings. Add a clasp, and you have a stunning bracelet.

● Single components, attached to a decorative earring finding, result in an eye-catching pair of earrings. Here, I've added a row of 3mm rings around the outside edge to keep the petals from flopping when they dangle from the earring finding.

● Be adventurous—make several components and experiment with other ways to combine them.

   You could, perhaps, connect them in a triangle shape for a pendant.

   You could alternate the Chrysanthemum component with another weave component— or with bead links.

   What if you punched holes in a leather or metal rectangle and connected components to it?

Play and have fun!

Love Knot Sparkle Necklace

This Raku triangle from Maku Studio has a wonderful texture with a blend of reflective rainbow colors. How could I do it justice? Well, wandering through a bead show, I spotted these sparkly, rainbow rondelles. A perfect start! Next, I decided to separate the beads with Love Knots and finish it with a magnetic clasp.

SKILL LEVEL: Beginner Plus

WEAVE: Love Knot

DIMENSIONS: 25-in. (64cm) necklace with a 2-in. (5cm) pendant

MATERIALS

JUMP RINGS

- **160** 16-gauge (AWG) 5.5mm I.D.
- **10** 16-gauge (AWG) 3mm I.D. (to connect the side chains and add the clasp)

WIRE

- 2 yd. (1.8m) 20-gauge wire, sterling silver

BEADS

- **20** 7x10mm faceted rondelles, rainbow finish
- **1** Raku pendant (Maku Studio)

FINDINGS

- **1** 8x14mm glue-on bail, rhodium plated pewter
- **1** 10x18mm pinch bail, sterling silver
- **1** magnetic clasp, fan shape, locking design, sterling silver (Star's Clasps)

OTHER SUPPLIES

- GS Hypo Bead Tip Cement or E6000 glue

TOOLS

- **2** pairs of pliers suitable for chain mail (flat nose, chainnose, bent nose)
- Pair of roundnose pliers to wire wrap the bead links
- Pair of flush cutters

Note: *The jump rings for this project were made from round, half-hard Argentium sterling silver wire. These ring sizes also work for Argentium sterling, 10% silver-filled, jeweler's bronze, or fully hardened copper jump rings. Choose your focal bead first, and then choose the accent beads that reflect the colors of the pendant bead.*

Plan of action

Make the Love Knot components

Wire-wrap the bead links

Add a glue-on bail to the pendant bead

Connect the Love Knots and the bead links

Attach the clasp

Join the side chains; add the pinch bail and pendant

Make adjustments

Explore & experiment

Make the Love Knot components

This necklace alternates Love Knot segments with wire-wrapped bead links. Follow the "Love Knot" weave instructions, p. 105, to make a knot. Repeat to make 20 knots in total. Each Love Knot component is about ½ in. (1.3cm) long **A**.

Wire-wrap the bead links

Wire-wrap the bead components (see "Wrapped loops," p. 8). Make 20 wire-wrapped bead links, each with one rondelle. Each loop must be large enough to hold two jump rings **B**.

Add a glue-on bail to the pendant bead

The Raku triangle did not come with a bail, which means you can control the materials used and the placement of the connecting bail.

The bail is glued onto the back of the pendant, so its loop extends just above the triangle. The pinch bail (added later) will connect to this bail. The photos show the glued-on bail added to the back of the pendant, and the loop that shows at the front **C, D**.

Connect the Love Knots and the bead links

With your pliers, open a ring at one side of a Love Knot, pass the open ring through the end loop of a bead link, and then close the ring. Now

open the second ring of the pair, add it to the same end loop, and close it. Open a ring at the other side of that Love Knot, pass the open ring through the loop at one end of another bead link, and then re-close the ring. Repeat with the second ring of that pair.

Continue to alternate each Love Knot with another bead link until you have a chain with 10 Love Knots and 10 bead links **E**. Repeat to make a second chain.

A

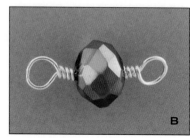

B

C

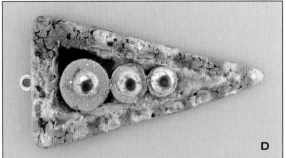

D

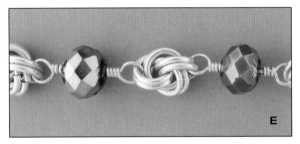

E

F

Attach the clasp

Open the two 16-gauge 3mm jump rings. Connect the bead link at the end of one chain to one side of the clasp (red dots). Repeat with the other side chain and the other side of the clasp **F**.

Join the side chains; add the pinch bail and pendant

The next step is to create the short, center-front, section of chain that connects the two side chains and provides a spot for the pendant to sit. Open the eight jump rings. Starting at an end Love Knot: Insert one ring through a pair of rings and close it (red dot). Add three pairs of rings (two rings into two rings). Slide on the bail over this chain. Use a ring to connect the mini chain to the Love Knot at the end of the other side chain.

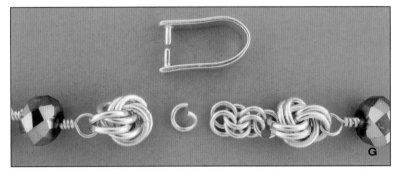

G

To add the pendant, use chainnose pliers to open the bail gently by exerting pressure inside the bail (so you don't mark the outer side). Slip the prongs into the loop of the glued on bail of the pendant, and then press it closed so the prongs touch **G**.

Make adjustments

The necklace can be made longer by adding Love Knot components, one on each side, next to the clasp.

Each Love Knot measures ½ in. (1.3cm), so adding a pair of knots adds 1 in. to the length. A Love Knot and a bead link measures 1¼ in. (3.2cm), so adding this pair to each side of the necklace adds 2½ in. (6.4cm) to the length. Of course, the necklace can be made shorter by adding fewer bead links and fewer Love Knots. You can make a smaller adjustment by adding one or two extra jump rings just before each half of the clasp.

Explore & experiment

For a simple bracelet, make a single chain of Love Knots and add a clasp. Add a single bead link at the center of the chain if you wish—or alternate knots and bead links as you did for the necklace. For earrings, add a single Love Knot to an earring finding, and then finish it off with a drop bead. Make the drop beads using the rondelles with headpins to make the wire wrap.

Ode to Bisbee Necklace

This necklace started with a visit to Bisbee, Arizona, a fascinating town with an interesting history. It's the home of copper mines and a vibrant artistic community, and this focal bead by Kate Drew Wilkinson combines those traditions. I used a variety of accent beads in copper, black, and red tones to make bead links that blend with the colors of the focal bead. The links are separated by chain mail knots made from copper jump rings.

SKILL LEVEL: Beginner Plus

WEAVE: Chinese Knot (Pheasible weave)

DIMENSIONS: 36 in. (.9m) necklace with a 2¾-in. (7cm) pendant

MATERIALS
JUMP RINGS
- **220** 18-gauge (AWG) 3.25mm I.D.
- **1** 18-gauge (AWG) 6mm I.D. (to add the drop bead to pendant)

WIRE
- Approx. 4 ft. (1.22m) 20-gauge wire, copper

Note: *The jump rings for this project were made from round, fully hardened copper wire. Use 3mm ID rings with Argentium sterling, 10% silver filled or jeweler's bronze wire. Choose accent beads that pull the colours from the "main event" bead (or ones that contrast with and enhance that bead).*

BEADS
- **2** 25x17x10mm oval beads, black glass
- **8** 9mm round beads, red coral
- **4** 8mm round beads, goldstone
- **2** 6mm round beads, goldstone
- **2** 8mm round beads, black onyx
- **2** 6mm round beads, black onyx
- **32** 6x3mm faceted edge rondelles, black (glass or onyx)
- **36** 4mm bicone crystals, jet (Swarovski)
- **1** 30x27mm pendant/focal bead (Kate Drew Wilkinson)
- **1** 30mm drop bead, coral, jet (Swarovski)

FINDINGS
- **2** small copper bead caps
- **1** 9x15mm copper snap clasp (ball-and-socket or trailer-hitch)

TOOLS
- **2** pairs of pliers suitable for chain mail (flatnose, chainnose, bentnose)
- Roundnose pliers
- Flush cutters
- Fine-tip permanent marker

Plan of action
- Make the Chinese Knot components
- Wire-wrap the bead links
- Wire-wrap the pendant bead and add the drop
- Connect the knots, the bead links, and the pendant bead
- Attach the clasp
- Make adjustments
- Explore & experiment

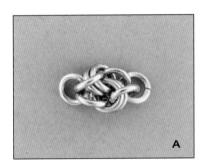

A

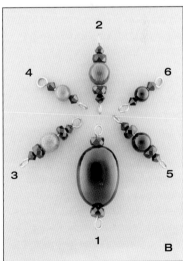

B

Make the Chinese Knot components

The necklace is built with Chinese Knot segments that alternate with bead components. Each Chinese Knot uses 10 jump rings. Follow the "Chinese Knot" weave instructions, p. 96, and then repeat to make 22 components in total. Each Chinese Knot is about ½ in. (1.3cm) long **A**.

Wire-wrap the bead links

I used seven different bead combinations to make a total of 21 bead links in this necklace:

1. Big black bead with two black rondelles (make two)
2. 9mm red bead with two black rondelles and two black bicones (make eight)
3. 8mm goldstone bead with two black rondelles and two black bicones (make four)
4. 6mm goldstone bead with two black bicones (make two)
5. 8mm black bead with two black rondelles and two black bicones (make two)
6. 6mm black bead with two black bicones (make two)

Experiment with craft wire to find the "right" length of wire needed to make a test bead link. Make the loops at each end similar in size to the 3mm jump rings. Use a fine-tip permanent marker to mark the sweet spot on your roundnose pliers. Unwind the loops and measure the length of the wire piece. The wire length to wrap my bead link 2, for example, measured 1¾ in. (4.4cm) long. Make a simple loop and center it (see "Simple loops, p. 7). String the beads for that bead link. Finish with another simple loop, and center it. Repeat for the bead links in this order: 2, 4, 6, 3, 5, 1 **B**.

C

Wire-wrap the pendant bead and add the drop

To wrap the pendant bead, first estimate the length of wire you'll need. Make a simple loop at one end. Add a bead cap, the focal bead, and the other bead cap. Finish with a wrapped loop (see "Wrapped loops," p. 8). Use a jump ring to add the drop bead to the simple loop at the bottom of the pendant **C**. (I used an 18-gauge 6mm jump ring.)

Connect the knots, the bead links, and the pendant bead

Organize the bead links into six piles, 1–6, as described earlier. Each Chinese Knot you made is going to alternate with one of these bead links. Starting with the pendant bead, you will build two identical, separate side chains. Set out the components for the first side chain:

D

- Chinese Knot, bead link 1
- Chinese Knot, bead link 2
- Chinese Knot, bead link 3
- Chinese Knot, bead link 2
- Chinese Knot, bead link 4
- Chinese Knot, bead link 5
- Chinese Knot, bead link 2,
- Chinese Knot, bead link 6
- Chinese Knot, bead link 3
- Chinese Knot, bead link 2
- Chinese Knot

With your pliers, open the ring at one end of the first Chinese Knot, pass the open ring through the top loop of the pendant bead, and then

close the ring. Open the ring at the other end of that Chinese Knot, pass the open ring through the loop at one end of bead link 1, and then re-close the ring. Continue to alternate a knot with the next bead link, following the order of links and knots listed above **D, E**.

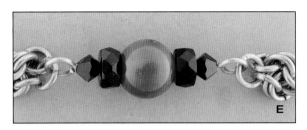

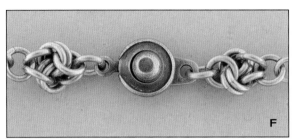

Attach the clasp

Open the end ring of a Chinese Knot at one end of your chain, pass the open ring through the loop of one half of your snap clasp, and then close the ring **F**. Repeat to add the other end of your chain to the other half of your snap clasp. The photos show the front and back of the clasp **G**.

Make adjustments

The necklace can be made longer by adding additional Chinese Knot components in pairs, one on each side, next to the clasp. Use a ring to connect the ends of two knots together. Each pair will add 1 in. (2.5cm) to the length. Each Chinese Knot requires 10 additional jump rings.

Explore & experiment

For a simple bracelet, make a single chain of Chinese Knots and add a clasp. Add one bead link at the center of a bracelet. Or, make a three-strand bracelet with three strands of linked Chinese Knots, using a multi-strand clasp to finish it off. Use an extra jump ring to join one Chinese Knot to the next Chinese Knot. For earrings, add a single Chinese Knot to an earring finding, and then finish it off with a drop bead. A Swarovski jet coral drop would look amazing!.

Parallel Purple Necklace

I found some beautiful purple stones at a gem show. They came in different sizes, they were faceted, and as a bonus, they weren't expensive! I decided I wanted to feature them in an asymmetric design. I chose the Parallel (Helm) weave to make both delicate chains and chunky chains. The final touch was to combine the purple beads with sterling saucer beads, each in two sizes.

SKILL LEVEL: Beginner Plus

WEAVE: Parallel (Helms)

DIMENSIONS: 23 in. (58cm) necklace with a 2½-in. (6.4cm) pendant

MATERIALS
JUMP RINGS
- **179** 20-gauge (AWG) 5mm I.D. (large)
- **144** 20-gauge (AWG) 3.5mm I.D. (small)
- **23** 16-gauge (AWG) 7mm I.D. (large)
- **19** 16-gauge (AWG) 4.25mm I.D. (small)

WIRE
- 15 in. (38cm) 20-gauge wire

BEADS
- **3** 16mm round, faceted beads, purple semi-precious
- **4** 10mm round, faceted beads, purple semi-precious
- **6** 12mm Bali saucer beads, sterling silver
- **2** 8mm Bali saucer beads, sterling silver

FINDINGS
- **1** 14mm lobster clasp, sterling silver

TOOLS
- **2** pairs of pliers suitable for chain mail (flatnose, chainnose, bentnose)
- Pair of roundnose pliers
- Pair of flush cutters

Note: *The jump rings for this project are made from round, Argentium sterling silver wire. The 20-gauge wire is half-hard, and the 16-gauge wire is soft. These ring sizes also work for 10% silver-filled, copper or jeweler's bronze jump rings.*

Plan of action
Wire-wrap the bead components
....
Make two long 20-gauge chains
....
Make two short 16-gauge chains
....
Connect the side components
....
Adjust the side lengths
....
Make and add the two back chains
....
Attach the clasp
....
Explore & experiment

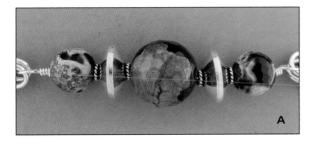

A

B

Wire-wrap the bead components
Make two identical bead links with wrapped loops (see "Wrapped loops," p. 8). Use two small stone beads, one large stone bead, and two large saucer beads **A**. Make the beaded pendant with wrapped loops. Use one large stone bead, two large saucer beads, and two small saucer beads **B**.

Make two long 20-gauge chains
Use the two sizes of 20-gauge jump rings to create two chains (see "Parallel" weave instructions, p. 106), one with 22 pattern repeats and another with 23 pattern repeats **C**. To count

the number of repeats, just count the number of pairs of small rings in your length of chain.

Make two short 16-gauge chains
Use the two sizes of 16-gauge jump rings to create two chains, one with only one pattern and another with four pattern repeats **D**.

Connect the side components
For the side with 20-gauge chains:
- Add two small 20-gauge rings to a loop of the beaded pendant. Next, open a large 16-gauge ring, and pick up those two rings and the two rings at the end of both

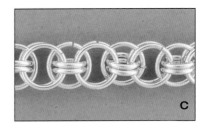

C

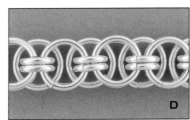

D

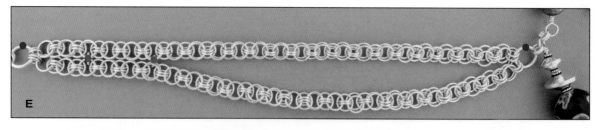

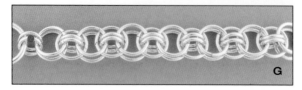

long chains (six small rings in all). Close the large ring (blue dot).
- Open a large 16-gauge ring, and pick up the four small rings at the other ends of the long chains. Close the large ring (blue dot). Make sure the chains are not twisted.
- Open two small 20-gauge rings. Use one ring to join the pairs of large rings, in each chain, that are third from the end (red dot).
- Use the second ring to join the pairs of large rings, in each chain, that are sixth from the end (red dot) **E**. (These joins will help the chains to sit side-by-side when worn.)

For the side with the bead links:
- Open two small 20-gauge rings. Hold an open ring, pick up the top loop (blue dot) of the pendant and a loop of a bead link. Close the ring. Repeat with the second ring.
- Open two small 16-gauge rings.

Hold an open ring, pick up the other end (red dot) of the bead link and the pair of large rings at the end of the shortest 16-gauge chain. Close the ring. Repeat with the second ring.
- Repeat the previous step to connect the other end of the short chain (green dot) to the second bead link.
- Repeat again to connect the other end of the bead second bead link (turquoise) to the longer chain (four pattern repeats).
- Open two small and one large 16-gauge rings. Add the two small rings, and then the large ring to the end of this chain (yellow dot) **F**.

Adjust the side lengths

Depending on the sizes of your beads links, you may need to adjust the length of your side chains. You want each side of the necklace to be approximately the same length.

Make the back chains

Use the two sizes of 20-gauge rings to make two Parallel weave chains, each with six pattern repeats. Open four small 20-gauge rings. Use two small rings to connect each back chain to the large 16-gauge ring at the end of each side chain (red dot) **G**.

Attach the clasp

Decide which way you want to wear this necklace. If you want the side with the two chains on the right, and you are right-handed, attach the clasp on that side of the necklace: Use two small 20-gauge rings to connect it to the end pair of rings; on the other end of the necklace, use two small 20-gauge rings to add a large 16-gauge ring (red dots) **H**. The lobster clasp will connect to this ring when you wear the necklace.

Explore & experiment

A bracelet could be a single length of heavy chain with a clasp, or it could be multiple strands linked side to side. Or, it could have a bead link as a focal point. Earrings can be short and heavy or long and delicate, depending on the ring gauge. Finish them off with crystal drops or charms.

Sweet Chrysacolla Necklace

This stunning pendant by Deb Benninger, a wire artist located in the Toronto area, demanded a special setting. The turquoise-blue shades of chrysacolla radiate calm—and I was very happy to find some matching beads at a gem show. I chose the Sweetpea weave to combine with the bead link components.

SKILL LEVEL: Intermediate

WEAVE: Sweetpea

DIMENSIONS: 17 in. (43cm) necklace with a 1¾-in. (4.4cm) pendant

MATERIALS
JUMP RINGS
- **348** 20-gauge (AWG) 3.25mm I.D.

WIRE
- 21 in. (53cm) 20-gauge wire, sterling silver

Note: The jump rings for this project were made from round, Argentium sterling silver wire. These ring sizes also work for 10% silver-filled or jeweler's bronze jump rings.

BEADS
- **8** 10x10x5mm chiclet Crysacolla beads (Voices of the Stones)
- **26** 6x4mm rondelle Crysacolla beads (Voices of the Stones)
- **1** wire-wrapped Chrysacolla pendant (Deb Benninger, I.D. Jewelry and Design)

FINDINGS
- **2** 2-to-1 strand reducers (or multi-strand connectors)
- **1** 12mm toggle clasp, sterling silver (bar 20mm)

TOOLS
- **2** pairs of pliers suitable for chain mail (flatnose, chainnose, bentnose)
- Pair of roundnose pliers
- Pair of flush cutters

Plan of action

Wire wrap the bead links
....
Make the Sweetpea chain components
....
Build the side chains and back chains
....
Connect the side chains to the back chains
....
Decide how to connect to the pendant
....
Attach the clasp
....
Explore & experiment

A

B

C

D

E

Wire-wrap the bead links
Make four bead links with simple loops (see "Simple loops," p. 7), using one chiclet stone bead per link **A**.

Make four bead links with simple loops using one chiclet and four rondelle stone beads per link **B**.

Make four bead links with simple loops using one rondelle per link **C**.

Make two bead links with simple loops using three rondelles per link **D**.

Make the Sweetpea components
See the "Sweetpea" weave instructions, p. 109. Using the 20-gauge 3.25mm jump rings: Make six lengths of chain, each with five units (A chains), and make four lengths of chain, each with seven units (B chains) **E**.

Build the side chains and back chains
Outer Side Chains: Set out a B bead link, an A chain, an A bead link, an A chain, and a B bead link. Use your pliers to carefully open the loop at the end of the C bead-link (just like opening a jump ring), add on the end jump ring of the A chain, and re-close the loop. Repeat this strategy to build the side chain in the order given above. Repeat to build another side chain.

Inner Side Chains: Set out a C bead link, a B chain, a D bead link, a B chain, and a C bead link. Use the previous technique to build the first inner side chain; connect the elements in the order above. Repeat to make the second inner chain **F**.

Back Chains: Set out an A chain and an A bead link. Use the previous technique to build the first back chain. Repeat to make the second back chain.

Connect the side chains to the back chains
Set out a 2-to-1 strand reducer, a back chain, and a jump ring. Open the jump ring, add the one-loop side of the finding, add the end jump ring of the back chain, and close the

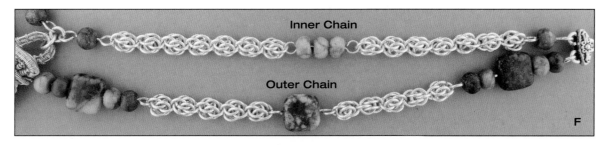

Inner Chain

Outer Chain

F

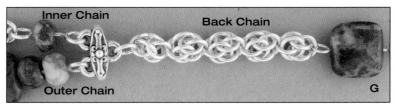

Inner Chain

Back Chain

Outer Chain

G

H

I

ring. Repeat to connect the other back chain to the other finding. Set out an inner side chain, an outer side chain, and a back chain. Open the end loop of a bead link in a side chain, and add it to one of the two remaining loops of the finding. Repeat with the other side chain.

Repeat to add the other two side chains to the other back chain **G**.

Decide how to connect to the pendant

This step is tricky because it depends on what the back side of your pendant looks like—you may need to improvise. My pendant came with a built-in wire loop. I found a jump ring large enough to go around that loop. Then I used a second jump ring to gather up the ends of the two inner chains and

the jump ring around the pendant loop. Next, I had to find two spots on the back of the pendant and on either side of that wire-wrapped loop. I opened the loop at the end of each bead link, inserted the loop through a wire on the back of the pendant, and closed the loop. This step took some experimentation **H**.

Attach the clasp

Begin with the ring half of the toggle clasp: Use a jump ring to connect the end loop of the bead link to the loop on the ring half. For the bar, start at the end loop of the bead link and make a mini-chain with three jump rings. Before closing the third ring, add the loop of the bar **I**.

Make adjustments

Because it may be challenging to attach all four chains to a unique pendant, you may need to make adjustments to the chain lengths. Your goal is to make the inner and outer chains lie correctly when worn. Making the necklace longer or shorter is easy—just add or remove the same number of Sweetpea units from the each back chain.

Explore & experiment

The Sweetpea weave is one of my favorites. It can be made dainty or chunky, depending on the gauge of the wire. You can alternate the metal or the color from one unit or group of units to the next. Enjoy playing with this weave! Use different metals and connect sections with pearls, glass beads, metal beads, or gemstones in bead links.

Viper Basket Earrings

In late March, 2017, 18 members of Wild West Bead Society in Arlington, Texas were my student testers for this project. We had a great evening at Wild Beads making these delightful earrings—everyone loved them.

Plan of action

Make the two viper basket components

....

Add each chain to an earring wire

....

Add the top large ring

....

Add the bottom large ring and beads

....

Explore & experiment

SKILL LEVEL: Beginner

WEAVE: Viper Basket

DIMENSIONS: 1¼ in. (3.2cm), including the bead

MATERIALS

JUMP RINGS
- **28** 20-gauge (AWG) 3.5mm I.D.
- **14** 20-gauge (AWG) 5.5mm I.D.

BEADS
- **2** mini-pebble beads (Unicorne Beads)

FINDINGS
- **1** pair of earring findings, gold (wires, posts, or lever backs)

TOOLS
- **2** pairs of pliers suitable for chain mail (flatnose, chainnose, bentnose)
- Paper clip

Note: The jump rings for this project were made from round jeweler's bronze wire. These ring sizes also work for Argentium sterling, 10% silver-filled, or copper jump rings.

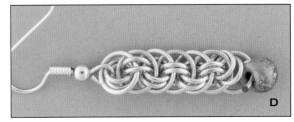

Make the viper basket components

Start by using the small rings to make a chain of two rings into two rings into two rings (see the "Viper Basket" weave instructions, p. 110) until you have a chain of seven pairs. Next, add large, overlapping, orbital rings to this chain (red dots): Open seven large rings, and follow "Add the large rings" **A**.

Add each chain to an earring wire

Remove the paper clip and replace it with an earring wire. There are two ways to do this: You can re-open the end pair of rings, one by one, add the loop of the earring wire to the jump ring, and re-close it—or you can treat the loop of the earring wire as if it were a jump ring. Hold the earring wire upside down and use your pliers to open the loop, Slide the open loop through the end pair of jump rings of your chain, then use your pliers to close the loop of the earring wire **B**.

Add the top large ring

Turn the chain so the first large ring is in front of all the rest. Hold an open, large ring in your pliers. Insert it front to back through the earring wire loop, and back to front through the second pair of small rings, and close it (red dot). This ring will sit in front of the next large ring **C**.

Add the bottom large ring and beads

Take the last large open ring, add a pebble bead, insert it through the second from last pair of small rings, and close it (red dot). It will follow the stacking order of the preceding large rings at the bottom of the earring **D**. Repeat to make another earring.

Explore & experiment

The Viper Basket weave makes a beautiful bracelet—either all in one metal, or with one metal for the small rings and other for the large ones. For a bracelet, I use 18-gauge 4.5mm and 7mm jump rings. One earring could be a zipper pull; just change out the earring wire for a lobster clasp.

Möbius Drop Earrings

So classic and elegant, the Möbius is another of my favorite weaves because of its infinite possibilities. (See "Yin Yang Necklace," p. 73, as an example.) Crystal bicones add the final, sparkling touch. These are fast to make and perfect to take as a hostess gift.

SKILL LEVEL: Beginner

WEAVE: Möbius

DIMENSIONS: 1 in. (2.5cm) earring

MATERIALS

JUMP RINGS

- **12** 18-gauge (AWG) 6mm I.D. (large)
- **10** 18-gauge (AWG) 4mm I.D. (small)
- **2** 20-gauge (AWG) 4mm I.D. (for crystals)

BEADS

- **2** 6mm crystal AB bicone crystals, top-drilled (Swarovski)

FINDINGS

- **1** pair of earring findings, silver (wires, posts, lever backs)

TOOLS

- **2** pairs of pliers suitable for chain mail (flatnose, chainnose, bentnose)

Note: The jump rings for this project were made from round, Argentium sterling wire. These ring sizes also work for jeweler's bronze, 10% silver-filled, or copper jump rings.

Plan of action

Make the two Möbius components

Add an earring wire and crystal to each Möbius

Explore & experiment

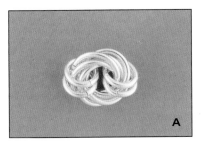

Make the Möbius components

A chain mail Möbius is a nest of rings where every ring passes through every other ring. The ones in these earrings are made with six large rings. The nests are locked and linked with small rings in pairs. Follow the "Möbius" weave instructions, p. 105, to make two Möbius components **A**.

Add an earring wire and crystal to each Möbius

Open a small ring, and add the earring wire and two small rings on the Möbius component. Close the ring. The 20-gauge rings will fit through the holes in the crystals. Open these two rings, add a crystal to one ring, and thread it through the other pair of small rings on one earring. Close the ring **B**, **C**. Repeat to make another earring.

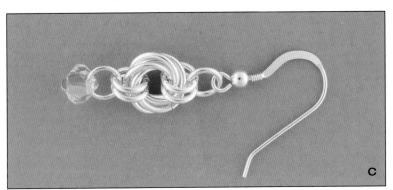

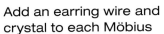

Explore & experiment

To make a simple bracelet, link a series of components together using two more small rings as connectors. Experiment with different sizes, colors, and numbers of rings—there's no rule that says a Möbius must have six rings.

Orchid Zipper Pull

The Orchid is a lovely, lacy, feminine weave. This zipper pull could be converted to make swingy earrings, or act as a pendant on a neck chain. It's easy to make it shorter or longer, and you can change the look by adding a different charm or drop bead.

Plan of action

Start with the lobster clasp and add the Orchid segments

....

Add a milagro heart drop

....

Explore & experiment

SKILL LEVEL: Beginner

WEAVE: Orchid

DIMENSIONS: 2½ in. (6.4cm), including the clasp

MATERIALS
JUMP RINGS
- **20** 18-gauge (AWG) 4.5mm I.D. (large)

FINDINGS
- **1** Milagro heart drop, antiqued gold (TierraCast)
- **1** 15mm lobster clasp, gold-plated

TOOLS
- **2** pairs of pliers suitable for chain mail (flatnose, chainnose, bentnose)

Note: *The jump rings for this project were made from jeweler's bronze wire. These ring sizes also work for Argentium sterling, 10% silver-filled, or copper.*

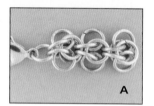

A

B

Start with the lobster clasp and add the Orchid segments

Follow the "Orchid" weave instructions, p. 106. Instead of using a twist tie, add the first ring to the loop on the lobster clasp. Repeat until you have two segments, then follow only steps 2 and 3 of a third segment **A**.

Add a milagro heart drop

Use a ring to add the heart: Open a ring, insert it through the loop on your drop, and through the last two rings at the base of ring your chain. Close the ring **B**.

Explore & experiment

Use 20-gauge 3.5mm I.D. jump rings for a more delicate chain. To make a simple bracelet, follow the Orchid weave instructions make a longer chain, and then add a clasp. Experiment with different metals and colors. You could use one color for the upright pairs of rings down the middle, and another for the rings that lie flat.

Parallel Zipper Pull

Where could you use this? On a jacket, a purse, your keys, a neck chain—or anything you can clip a lobster to. This is also a fast-to-make, creative addition to a gift. It can be personalized in many ways with different metals or meaningful charms.

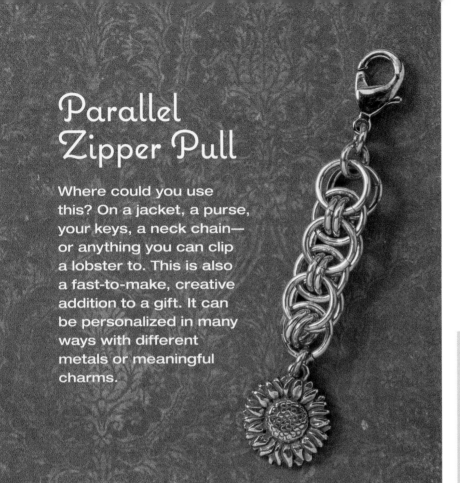

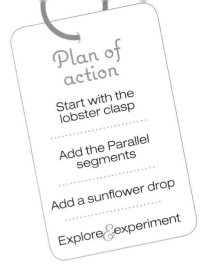

Plan of action

Start with the lobster clasp

Add the Parallel segments

Add a sunflower drop

Explore & experiment

SKILL LEVEL: Beginner

WEAVE: Parallel (Helm)

DIMENSIONS: 2¾ in. (7cm) long, including the lobster

MATERIALS

JUMP RINGS
- 9 16-gauge (AWG) 7mm I.D. (large)
- 7 16-gauge (AWG) 4.25mm I.D. (medium)
- 2 16-gauge (AWG) 3mm I.D. (small)

FINDINGS
- 1 sunflower drop, antiqued copper (TierraCast)
- 1 15mm lobster clasp, copper

TOOLS
- 2 pairs of pliers suitable for chain mail (flatnose, chainnose, bentnose)

Note: The jump rings for this project were made from fully hardened copper wire. These ring sizes also work for Argentium sterling or jeweler's bronze.

Start with the lobster clasp

Open a small jump ring. Insert it through the small ring on the clasp, and close the ring. Open a medium jump ring, insert it through the small ring you just added, and close it **A**.

Make the parallel component

Follow the "Parallel" weave instructions, p. 106. Instead of using a twist tie, build your chain on the starter piece you just completed. Make three Parallel units, but do not add the final pair of large jump rings **B**.

Add sunflower drop

Open a small ring, insert it through the loop on your drop and through the large ring at the end of your chain, and close the ring **C**.

A

B

C

Explore & experiment

To make a simple bracelet, follow the Parallel weave steps to make a longer chain, and then add a clasp. Experiment with different metals and colors. You could use one color for the small rings, and another for the medium ones. You could make a bracelet more delicate with 18-gauge 6mm (or 6.25mm) and 4mm rings; or even more so with 20-gauge 5mm and 3.5mm rings.

Byzantine Windows Necklace

This is one of the first chain mail necklaces I ever made. Since then, I've made several variations of it—and it has always been a design that attracts comments. Best of all, it's easy to make!

Plan of action

Make the Byzantine components

Wire-wrap the crystals with the headpins

Connect the chain components and the crystals

Attach the clasp

Make adjustments

Explore & experiment

SKILL LEVEL: Beginner Plus

WEAVE: Byzantine

DIMENSIONS: 15½ in. (39.4cm) necklace

MATERIALS
JUMP RINGS
- **572** 18-gauge (AWG) 3.5mm I.D.
- **1** 16-gauge (AWG) 3mm I.D.
- **1** 16-gauge (AWG) 5mm I.D.

BEADS
- **14** 6mm round crystals (#5000 Swarovski)

FINDINGS
- **14** 1½-in. (3.8cm) headpins, sterling silver, ball end
- **1** 14mm lobster clasp, sterling silver

TOOLS
- **2** pairs of pliers suitable for chain mail (flatnose, chainnose, bentnose)
- Pair of roundnose pliers
- Pair of flush cutters

Note: *The jump rings for this project were made from regular sterling silver wire. These ring sizes also work for Argentium sterling, 10% silver-filled, copper, or jeweler's bronze jump rings. Choose your favorite color of Swarovski crystals—I've used crystal AB, the sapphire blue in the photo, rose, and white opal.*

A

B

C

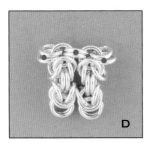

D

E

Make the Byzantine components

Follow the instructions for the "Byzantine" weave, p. 91. Make 26 single segments, and make two chains, each with 3½ segments **A, B**. These are the back chains.

Wire-wrap the crystals with the headpins

Use a headpins to wrap each crystal (see "Simple loops," p. 7). I used 1¼ in. (3.2cm) to wrap a crystal, so you can clip off the excess either before you wrap or after. My loops were about 3mm I.D.—a bit smaller than the jump rings **C**.

Connect the chain components and crystals

Set out the 26 single Byzantine segments. Open 78 rings, and set them out in rows of six. Join two Byzantine segments together. Link the top two rings of each with a pair of rings, add two rings to the top of the left segment, and add two rings

to the top of the right segment (red dots) **D**. Repeat to make 13 pairs of segments.

Set out the 14 crystals. Open 14 jump rings. With one open ring, scoop up the side of one Byzantine pair, a bead loop, and the side of another segment pair (red dot). Continue to add the crystals in between the Byzantine pairs **E**. Finish by adding a crystal to each end of this center section.

Next, you will add the back chains: Open four rings. Use two rings to connect the crystal at one end of the center section to a back chain (red dot) **F**. Repeat on the other side to add the other back chain.

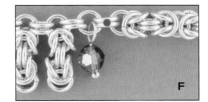

F

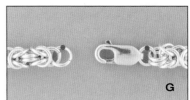

G

Attach the clasp

Open the 16-gauge 3mm ring, and add the lobster clasp and the pair of rings at one end of your chain. Close the ring. Open the 16-gauge 5mm ring, and insert it through the pair of rings at the other end of your chain (red dots) **G**.

Make adjustments

The necklace can be made longer by adding additional half-Byzantine segments in pairs, one on each side, next to the clasp. Each pair will add ½ in. (1.3cm) to the length. Each half-segment requires six additional jump rings. Of course, the necklace can be made shorter by reducing the length of the back chains.

Explore & experiment

To make a bracelet, use the same crystals as the necklace—or use a 6mm round gemstone bead, such as onyx or amethyst. The bracelet is similar in construction to the necklace, except the beads have just a simple loop on both sides, and the base of the bracelet is connected to match the top edge. For earrings, make two continuous Byzantine segments, add to an earring finding, and then finish it off with a wire-wrapped crystal.

Beez Beads Necklace

I love beads of all kinds, whether they're crystals, gemstones, lampwork glass, or seed beads. So my personal challenge was to create a chain mail bead. This one was created with the Beez to Butterflies weave, a variation of the classic Byzantine weave. It looks best on a fairly rigid chain or neckpiece. I paired the chain mail with black, oval ceramic beads (made by Regaliz). It's a perfect combination that can be worn with both casual and dressy clothing.

SKILL LEVEL: Intermediate

WEAVE: Byzee Beez to Butterflies

DIMENSIONS: ¾ in. (1.9cm) x ½ in. (1.3cm) for each bead

MATERIALS (FOR THREE BEADS)

JUMP RINGS
- **216** 18-gauge (AWG) 4mm I.D.
- **12** 18-gauge (AWG) 6.5mm I.D. (temporary, in any metal)

BEADS
- **4** 10x19mm oval beads, shiny black ceramic (Regaliz)

FINDINGS
- **1** 15–18 in. neck chain or neck piece, silver

TOOLS
- **2** pairs of pliers suitable for chain mail (flatnose, chainnose, bentnose)

Note: The jump rings for this project were made from round, half-hard Argentium sterling silver wire. These ring sizes also work for 10% silver filled, jeweller's bronze, or copper. The beads look best on a wide, rigid or semi-rigid necklace—mine is shown on an 8mm wide, sterling silver Omega chain.

Plan of action

Make six mini-chains

Add temporary rings

Connect six segments side-by-side

Join the ends to make a bead

Make two more beads, and add to a neck chain

Explore & experiment

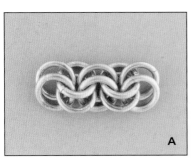

A

B

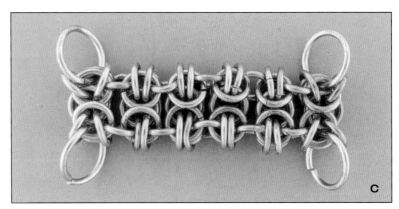

C

Make six mini-chains

The necklace uses three Beez Beads. Follow the "Byzee Beez to Butterflies" weave instructions, p. 94, to make six mini-chains **A**.

Add temporary rings

Follow the next few steps to fold and lock the mini-chain, with temporary rings to lock in the folded rings **B**.

Connect six segments side-by-side

Follow the remaining steps to connect the six segments side-by-side **C**. Remove the temporary rings.

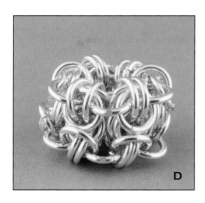

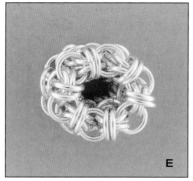

Join the ends to make a bead

The final step is to use two more open rings to connect the first segment to the last one—the same way you connected all the others (green dots) **D, E**.

Make two more beads and add to neck chain

Repeat the previous steps to make two more Beez Beads. Add the bead components to a neck chain, alternating with the black, ceramic Regaliz beads, and try it on!

Explore & experiment

Make and connect enough Byzee Beez segments to fit your wrist. Add a clasp, and you have a gorgeous bracelet.

Be adventurous—experiment with other weaves to see if you can create a bead. Start with an even number of segments, and be sure they are flexible enough to make a circle the right size. You also need to be able to join the two ends together. Two Chrysanthemum segments might make an interesting bead, for example.

If you create a bead you're happy about, please post a photo on my Marilyn Gardiner Design Facebook page to share it with others!

Oriental Beads Pendant

The idea of making small balls of woven chain mail is fascinating! So, I learned how to do that. Next, what to do with those balls? The first answer is to string them like beads—but then I had the idea of using these "beads" to build a pendant. I like the result, and I can think of many other ways to use these balls.

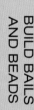

SKILL LEVEL: Intermediate

WEAVES: Japanese Ball and Inverted Roundmaille

DIMENSIONS 18 in. (46cm) necklace with 1½-in. (3.8cm) pendant

MATERIALS
JUMP RINGS
- **526** 22-gauge (AWG) 2.75mm I.D.
- **748** 20-gauge (AWG) 3.25mm I.D.

WIRE
- 10 in. (25cm) 20-gauge wire, gold

BEADS
- **2** 10mm round, corrugated beads, gold-filled
- **4** 6mm round disk spacer beads, gold

CLASP
- **1** 15x11mm magnetic box clasp, gold (Star's Clasps)

TOOLS
- **2** pairs of pliers suitable for chain mail (flatnose, chainnose, bentnose)
- Pair of roundnose pliers
- Pair of flush cutters

Note: The jump rings for this project were made from round, jeweler's bronze wire. These ring sizes also work for Argentium sterling and 10% silver-filled jump rings. Each Japanese Ball is about 13mm in diameter.

Plan of
action

Make the Japanese
Ball components

Make the Inverted
Roundmaille
side chains

Wire-wrap the
bead links

Connect the balls
to make the
pendant

Join the pendant,
bead links, and
side chains

Attach the clasp

Make adjustments

Explore&experiment

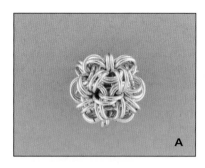

A

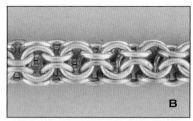

B

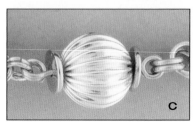

C

Make the Japanese Ball components

Japanese Balls are very ring-size sensitive. If the ball is loose, you can stuff extra rings inside before closing. If it is tight, you will have difficulty adding the last few jump rings. Each Japanese Ball uses 84 jump rings. Follow the "Japanese Ball," weave instructions, p. 103, using 22-gauge, 2.75mm jump rings, and make six Balls. Each Ball is about 13mm in diameter **A**.

Make Inverted Roundmaille side chains

This easy, fast-to-make chain is round and hollow. It uses three rings per pattern repeat. Follow the "Inverted Roundmaille" weave instructions, p. 101, using 20-gauge 3.25mm jump rings. Each side chain measures about 6¾ in. (17.1cm) and each has 62 pattern repeats **B**.

Wire-wrap the bead links

Make two bead links with double loops (see "Double loops," p. 9); use one 10mm bead and two smaller disk beads for each link **C**.

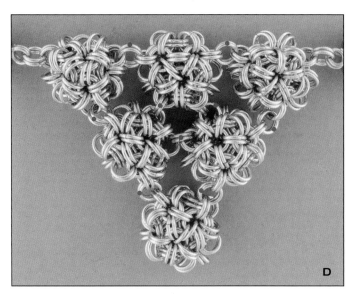

D

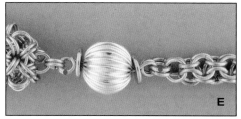

E

F

Connect the balls to make the pendant

Row 1

Each Ball will be connected to an adjacent Ball with two 22-gauge 2.75mm jump rings (see the red dots). Set out three Balls. Holding an open ring in your pliers, and add a pair of rings from one Ball and a pair of rings from another Ball. Close the ring. Add another ring beside that one (double up the ring). Add Ball 3 to the first pair. Start by picking up a pair of rings on Ball 2 that are directly opposite the previous connectors. Add any pair on Ball 3. and close it. Double up the ring.

Row 2

Connect Balls 4 and 5 with a pair of rings. Set these balls below the first row. Ball 4 will sit between Balls 1 and 2. You will connect Ball 4 to

both Balls. Use one ring for each connection. You will need to "eye-ball" the pairs of rings to be linked. Do the same to join Ball 5 to Balls 2 and 3. You may need to re-position the connecting rings. When you are happy with the look, double up those joining rings.

Row 3

Ball 6 will sit below and between Balls 4 and 5 and will be connected to both of them. Connect the top left side of the new ball to the base of Ball 4. Connect the top right side of the new ball to the base of Ball 5 **D**.

Join the pendant, bead links, and side chains

Use two 22-gauge 2.75mm rings to connect a top corner of the pendant to a bead link. Repeat to join the other corner to the other bead link (red dots) **E**.

Remove one ring from each end of both side chains. This tapers the chain so it ends in two rings. Use one of these rings to join the end of a chain to a bead link. Double up that ring. Repeat to join the other chain to the other bead link.

Use a 20-gauge 3.25mm ring to connect the end of a side chain to the loop on half of the clasp. Repeat to add the other side chain to the other half of the clasp (red dots) **F**.

Make adjustments

The necklace can be made longer by adding to the side chain. Each inch requires about 30 rings. To add an inch to each chain, you will need 60 rings. (This is 10 more repeats on each chain.)

Explore & experiment

Line the Balls all in a row as the center focus of a necklace, and let your imagination run wild! Before making them all, you can use felt balls to experiment with the arrangement. A bracelet of linked Balls would be amazing—but a lot of work! For earrings, insert a headpin through the Ball, make a simple loop, and then add it to an earring finding. You could also make a chain of Balls, dangling one below the other.

Trizantine Necklace

I love this square Swarovski crystal element, and I wanted to use it as a pendant. My solution was to make a circle of flat mesh. Next came the beads and chain. Round onyx beads looked amazing when paired with different sizes of Bali silver saucer beads. I wanted a square-looking chain because of the square pendant, so Trizantine turned out to be perfect.

SKILL LEVEL: Intermediate

WEAVES: Trizantine, European 4-in-1, and Byzantine

DIMENSIONS: 22½ in. (57.2cm) necklace with 1½ in. (3.8cm) pendant

MATERIALS

JUMP RINGS
- **332** 18-gauge (AWG) 4.5mm I.D.
- **159** 20-gauge (AWG) 2.8mm I.D.
- **18** 18-gauge (AWG) 3mm I.D. (for connectors)

WIRE
- 15 in. (38cm) 20-gauge wire, silver

BEADS
- **10** 8mm round beads, onyx
- **4** 12x8.5mm saucer beads, sterling silver
- **4** 8mm saucer beads, sterling silver
- **1** 30mm square bead, jet (#4439 Swarovski)

FINDINGS
- **1** 9mm square toggle clasp, sterling silver

TOOLS
- **2** pairs of pliers suitable for chain mail (flatnose, chainnose, bentnose)
- Pair of roundnose pliers
- Pair of flush cutters
- Piece of plastic needlepoint canvas #7 (seven holes/inch)

Notes: *The jump rings for this project were made from round, half-hard, silver-filled wire (10%). These ring sizes also work for Argentium sterling or jeweler's bronze jump rings.*

Plan of action

- Make the Trizantine components
- Make the European 4-in-1 bail
- Make a short Byzantine chain
- Wire-wrap the bead components
- Build the side chains
- Connect the side chains with Byzantine and add the bail
- Attach the clasp
- Make adjustments
- Explore & experiment

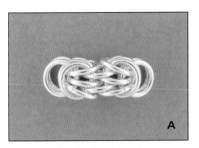

Make the Trizantine components

Follow the instructions for the "Trizantine" weave, p. 108, using 18-gauge 4.5mm jump rings. Make four chains with two segments. Make two chains with six segments **A**.

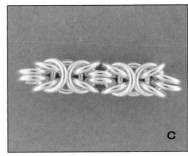

Make the European 4-in-1 bail

Follow the instructions for the "European 4-in-1" weave, p. 98, using 20-gauge 2.8mm jump rings, to make a rectangle. This chain starts with four pairs of rings connected by three single rings. Make a flat strip that has 19 edge rings. Insert the strip of chain through the Swarovski square jet bead. Use three rings to join the strip into a continuous loop. Follow the last two weave instructions **B**.

Make a short Byzantine chain

Follow the instructions for the "Byzantine" weave, p. 91, using 20-gauge 2.8mm jump rings. Make a chain with two segments **C**.

Wire-wrap the bead components

Use a 2½-in. (6.4cm) piece of 20-gauge wire to make six bead link components with a double loop at each end (see "Double loops," p. 9). Four links have an onyx bead, a large saucer bead, and an onyx bead **D**. Two links have a small saucer bead, an onyx bead, and a small saucer bead **E**.

Build the side chains

Set out in this order: a large saucer bead link, a two-segment Trizantine chain, a small saucer bead link, a two-segment Trizantine chain, a large saucer bead link, and a six-segment Trizantine chain. Use five connector 18-gauge 3mm jump rings to join these components into one chain. Repeat to make the other side chain **F**.

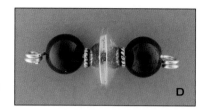

Connect the side chains with Byzantine and add the bail

Take the two-unit Byzantine chain, and use a 3mm ring to connect it to a large saucer bead link at one end of a side chain. Dangle that side chain and let the Byzantine section drop down through the loop of the bail. Push the bail to one side so you can use a 3mm ring to connect the end of the Byzantine section to a large saucer bead link at the end of the other side chain **G**.

Attach the clasp

Use a 3mm ring to attach the ring half of the clasp to one end of the necklace. Use three 3mm rings to make a one-in-one mini-chain that connects the bar half of the clasp to the other end of the necklace **H**.

Make adjustments

The necklace can be made longer by adding additional half Trizantine segments in pairs, one on each side, next to the clasp. Of course, the necklace can be made shorter by adding fewer units.

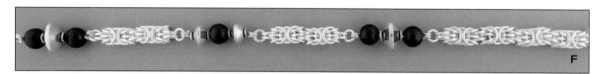

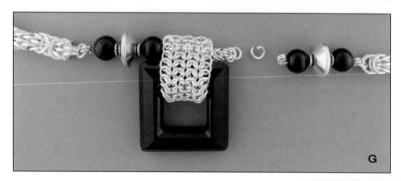

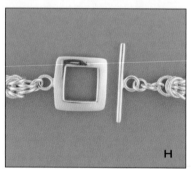

Explore & experiment

For a simple bracelet, make a small bead link with silver and onyz beads, and then add side chains in Trizantine plus a clasp. For earrings, add a Trizantine chain (one, two, or three links) to an earring finding. For a more delicate chain, use 20-gauge 3.75mm jump rings. Use a headpin to wrap a small black onyx bead to dangle from the base of the chain.

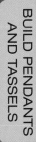

Byzantine
Star Pendant

I love this necklace. The star is easy
to make, and it's perfect for adding
your favorite pendant. This pendant
bead was made by polymer clay artist
Barbara Colautti. The side chains are
a simple two rings into two rings, so
it's easy to adjust the length.

SKILL LEVEL: Beginner Plus

WEAVES: Byzantine and 4-in-2

DIMENSIONS: 22 in. (56cm) necklace with 3-in. (7.6cm) pendant

MATERIALS
JUMP RINGS
- **402** 18-gauge (AWG) 3.5mm I.D. (small)
- **12** 18-gauge (AWG) 5mm I.D. (large)
- **2** 18-gauge (AWG) 5.5mm I.D.
- **1** 16-gauge (AWG) 4.5mm I.D.
- **1** 16-gauge (AWG) 3mm I.D.

BEADS
- **1** pendant bead with top loop (Barbara Colautti, Toronto)

CLASP
- **1** 15mm lobster clasp, sterling silver

TOOLS
- **2** pairs of pliers suitable for chain mail (flatnose, chainnose, bentnose

***Note:** The jump rings for this project were made from round, half-hard, Argentium sterling silver wire. These ring sizes also work for regular sterling, 10% silver-filled, jeweler's bronze, or copper jump rings. If your pendant does not come with a top loop, you will need a long headpin, and maybe some spacer beads or a bead cap for the top and bottom of your bead.*

Plan of action
Make the Byzantine chain
....
Make the star
....
Make the side chains and add the star and the pendant
....
Attach the clasp
....
Make adjustments
....
Explore&experiment

A

B

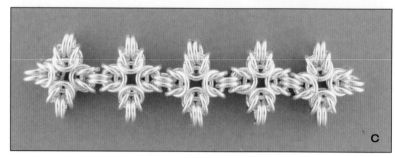

C

Make the Byzantine chain

Follow the "Byzantine" weave instructions, p. 91, using small rings, but in the third step, use two large rings to lock in the fold. Complete the segment using small rings. Repeat until the chain is five segments long **A**.

Go back to the first segment. Add two linked pairs of small rings to the top of the large center rings. Fold them and lock them in place with two more small rings. You have added half of a Byzantine segment **B**.

Repeat this step on the other side of this same pair of large rings. You have a vertical segment inter-locked with the horizontal one—it looks like a plus sign! Continue to add half-segments to the top and bottom of each pair of large rings in your chain **C**.

Make the star

Take a 5mm ring and pick up the five pairs of rings along the top of the chain. Close the ring (red dot). This will be tough to do; use pliers with fine tips. Now, add a second large ring in the same place **D**. This ring will also be a challenge to get closed. (If you can't close it, use two 5.5mm jump rings.)

Next, close the circle to complete the star. Where the end pairs touch (green dots, **D**), remove two of the small jump rings from one end. Open the two jump rings from the other end, and use them to connect the end pairs together to make a complete Byzantine segment (green dot) **E**.

Make the side chains, and add the star and pendant

Place two rings into two rings into two rings for the length of the sides (see "4-in-2" weave, p. 100) using 18-gauge 3.5mm jump rings. There are sufficient rings to make each side chain 10¼ in. (26cm) long (there are 73 pairs of rings in each side chain). Build the side chains from two adjacent points of the star. Alternatively, make the two side chains and then connect them to the stars. Use a heavier 16-gauge 3mm jump ring to attach the pendant at the base of the star **F**.

Attach the clasp

If the lobster clasp didn't come with a ring, use a small 18-gauge ring to pass through the loop on the lobster clasp and through the pair of rings at the end of a side chain. (If there is a closed/soldered ring attached to the lobster, re-open the last two rings of the chain to add the clasp.) Open the 16-gauge 4.5mm ring, and add it to the end of the other side chain. The lobster clasp will grab this ring to close the necklace **G**.

Make adjustments

The necklace can be made longer by adding pairs of rings to the side chains. Be sure to add the same number of pairs to each side. Of course, the necklace can be made shorter by removing pairs of rings from each side chain.

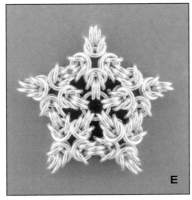

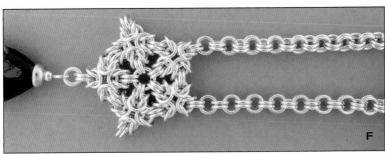

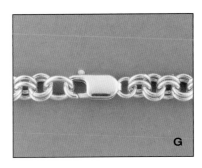

Explore & experiment

For a simple bracelet, make a chain of "plus signs" and add a clasp. For an earring, make a "plus sign" and add an earring finding. And of course, you can finish with a drop bead to coordinate with your pendant. Byzantine is a classic, and there are countless variations of this weave. Do some exploring on the Internet and find another variation that you'd like to try. (Trizantine, Olivia Byzantine, Byzantine Bias, Byzantine Filigree, Byzantine Knot, Byzantine Rose, Turtleback, and Atlantis are some examples.)

Byzantine Circle Pendant

This pendant features an outer ring of four Byzantine segments linked to an inner frame of two large, heavy jump rings. The Byzantine weave is a classic dating back to the Middle Ages. Many variations of Byzantine have been created to make today's jewelry.

SKILL LEVEL: Beginner

WEAVES: Byzantine and Jens Pind

DIMENSIONS: 17 in. (43cm) chain with 1½-in. (3.8cm) pendant

MATERIALS

JUMP RINGS
- **50** 16-gauge (AWG) 4.75mm I.D.
- **3** 14-gauge (AWG) 8mm I.D. (large)
- **8** 16-gauge (AWG) 4mm I.D. (connectors)
- **286** 18-gauge (AWG) 3mm I.D.

CLASP
- **1** toggle clasp, copper

TOOLS
- **2** pairs of pliers suitable for chain mail (flatnose, chainnose, bentnose)

Note: *The jump rings for this project were made from round, fully hardened copper wire. These ring sizes also work for Argentium sterling, 10% silver-filled, or jeweler's bronze jump rings.*

Plan of action

Make the Byzantine chain
....
Connect the parts to make a pendant
....
Make the neck chain
....
Attach the clasp
....
Add the pendant
....
Make adjustments
....
Explore & experiment

A

Make the Byzantine chain

See the "Byzantine" weave instructions, p. 91, and use 18-gauge 4.75mm jump rings to make a chain that is four segments long **A**.

Connect the parts to make a pendant

Remove one ring from each end of the chain. Next, open one of the single end rings, hook it into the other end of the chain (beside the single ring), and close the ring (red dot). Repeat with the other single ring **B**.

Open four connector 16-gauge 4mm rings. Add a ring to the pair of rings separating the first two segments. Continue to add a ring between each segment, all on the same side of the chain (red dots) **C**.

Open two 14-gauge 8mm large rings. Using your pliers, insert a large ring through the four connector rings, and close the ring (red dot). You will notice that the Byzantine circle has rolled around so the large ring sits inside the circle **D**.

B

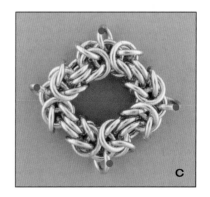

C

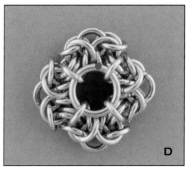

D

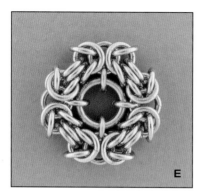

E

F

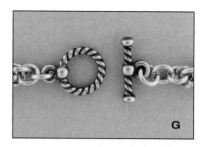

G

H

Add the second large ring through only three of the connector rings. (Do this because it's difficult to close that ring if you pass through all four connectors.) Now, reopen the fourth connector, add in the second large ring, and re-close the ring **E**. (This is a sneaky trick to solve a difficult problem!)

Make the neck chain
See the "Jens Pind" weave instructions, p. 104, and use 18-gauge 3mm jump rings to make a neck chain. Each repeat has three rings. Use 94 sets of three rings to make a 16¼ in. (41.3cm) chain, not including the clasp **F**.

Attach the clasp
Use a 3mm ring to attach the ring part of the clasp to one end of the neck chain. Use three 3mm rings to make a one-in-one mini-chain that connects the bar part of the clasp to the other end of the neck chain **G**.

Add the pendant
Rotate the Byzantine pendant so a connector ring is at the top of the center rings (green dot). Open four 16-gauge 4mm rings. Add two rings to the pair of Byzantine rings at the top of the pendant (above that connector ring). Add two rings into those two rings (red dots). Open the 14-gauge 8mm ring, and

add it to the last pair **H**. This large ring will allow you to pass a neck chain through the middle of this ring—just fold the bar part of the clasp and insert the chain.

Make adjustments
The neck chain can be made longer by adding additional pairs of rings to the chain. Each extra inch requires seven pairs of rings.

Explore & experiment

Make a three-strand bracelet with a Byzantine Circle as the centerpiece. The pendant is too heavy for an earring, but regular Byzantine chains would be light enough and look good with the pendant.

Princess Tassel

This necklace belongs to the young and the young-at-heart. A delicate and classic Byzantine chain is elevated with a sparkly, Byzantine tassel that can easily be removed as needed. It's perfect for both casual and dressier occasions.

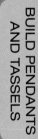

SKILL LEVEL: Beginner

WEAVE: Byzantine

DIMENSIONS: 19 in. (48cm) necklace with 4¼-in. (10.8cm) ring plus tassel

MATERIALS
JUMP RINGS
- **836** 20-gauge (AWG) 2.8mm I.D.
- **3** 18-gauge (AWG) 3.75mm I.D.
- **1** 16-gauge (AWG) 7mm I.D.
- **3** 18-gauge (AWG) 3mm I.D.
- **1** 18-gauge (AWG) 4.5mm I.D.

BEADS
- **8** 4mm bicone crystals **2** each of **4** colors (Swarovski)
- **3** 4x2.5mm convex cylinders, silver

FINDINGS
- **8** 1½-in. (3.8cm) 24-gauge headpins, sterling silver, 1.5mm ball end
- **1** 17mm hammered ring, silver (Via Murano)
- **1** 15mm lobster clasp, sterling silver

TOOLS
- **2** pairs of pliers suitable for chain mail (flatnose, chainnose, bentnose)
- Pair of roundnose pliers
- Pair of flush cutters

Note: The jump rings for this project were made from round, half-hard, Argentium sterling wire. These ring sizes also work for 10% silver-filled, jeweler's bronze, or copper jump rings. The hammered ring could have a different texture, or none, and can be smaller or larger in diameter. The silver beads at the tip of each tassel can vary as well—just be sure that you have jump rings to fit. The crystals can be top-drilled (so no need to wire-wrap); just add with a 20-gauge 4mm jump ring.

Plan of action

Make the Byzantine neck chain and tassel components

....

Wire wrap the crystals

....

Complete the tassel unit

....

Attach the clasp

....

Make adjustments

....

Explore & experiment

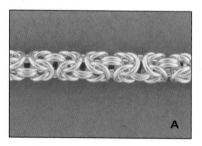

A

B

Make the Byzantine neck chain and tassel components

A single Byzantine segment uses 14 jump rings, and the following ones in a chain require 12 rings each. Follow the "Byzantine" weave instructions, p. 91, using 20-gauge 2.8mm jump rings. Make the neck chain 48 segments long. Make three tassel chains: a short one with five segments, a longer one with six and a half segments, and an even longer one with nine segments **A**.

Wire-wrap the crystals

String a crystal on a headpin, and use roundnose pliers to make a small wrapped loop (see "Wrapped loops," p. 8). Trim the wire. Repeat for all eight crystals **B**.

Complete the tassel unit

Use a pair of 20-gauge 2.8mm jump rings to add each of the three

tassel chains to the hammered silver ring. If the width of your ring is different than mine, you may need larger rings. Use 18-gauge 3.75mm jump rings to add a silver bead to the bottom tip of each tassel. Each ring will pass through the bead and through the end pair of rings of the tassel **C**.

Use 20-gauge 2.8mm rings to randomly add different colored crystals to the sides of the tassel chains. I added one to the short one, three to the longer one, and four to the longest one **D**.

Attach the clasp

If the lobster clasp didn't come with a ring through the loop, use an 18-gauge 3mm jump ring to pass through the loop on the lobster clasp. Close it. Use another 3mm ring to thread on the lobster ring and the pair of rings at one end of the neck chain.

At the other end of the neck chain, add a 3mm ring, and close it. Then add an 18-gauge 4.5mm jump ring through that one (red dots). This last ring will connect to the lobster to close the necklace. **E**

Make adjustments

The necklace can be made longer by adding additional Byzantine segments, next to the clasp. Each pair will add $^3/_8$ in. in. to the length. Each segment requires 12 additional jump rings. The tassel could have more crystals added. The crystals could be all one color, or a variety of colors.

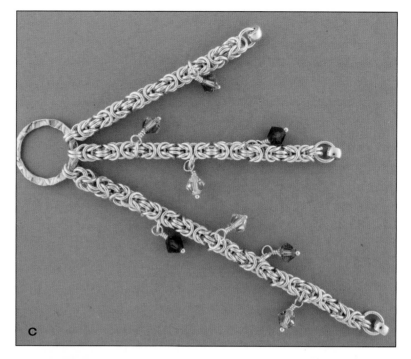

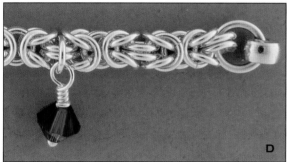

Explore & experiment

For a simple bracelet, make a single Byzantine chain and add a clasp. For a heavier chain, use 18-gauge 3.5mm rings or 16-gauge 4.5mm rings. You can also use a bead cap to hold the tassels. For earrings, just make Byzantine chains to your desired length, and add wire-wrapped bicone crystals or silver drop beads at the ends.

Tassels and Pearls Necklace

This one all started because I wanted to make a long necklace with a full tassel. This one is its third reincarnation—I was trying to make it pleasing to me, but also have a bit of pizzazz.

SKILL LEVEL: Beginner Plus

WEAVE: Byzantine

DIMENSIONS: 28 in. (71cm) necklace with a 4-in. (10cm) tassel unit

MATERIALS

JUMP RINGS
- **436** 18-gauge (AWG) 3.5mm I.D.
- **380** 20-gauge (AWG) 2.8mm I.D.
- **2** 16-gauge (AWG) 3mm I.D.

WIRE
- 4 in. (10cm) 20-gauge wire

BEADS
- **7** 8mm crystal pearls, iridescent green (Swarovski)
- **2** 8mm crystal pearls, bright gold (Swarovski)
- **10** 6mm crystal pearls, antique brass (Swarovski)

FINDINGS
- **19** 2-in. (5cm) headpins, brass (TierraCast)
- **4** 10mm hammered links, gold-plated (TierraCast)
- **1** 9x11mm corrugated bead cone, vermeil
- **1** 9x15mm snap clasp, gold-plated

TOOLS
- **2** pairs of pliers suitable for chain mail (flatnose, chainnose, bentnose)
- Pair of roundnose pliers
- Pair of flush cutters

Note: The jump rings for this project were made from round, jeweler's bronze wire. These ring sizes also work for Argentium sterling, 10% silver-filled, or copper jump rings. I recommend that you choose your colors/sizes of pearls and findings so they complement your choice of metal color. And instead of using a spool of wire to wrap the beads, I used extra headpins (just clip off the ends).

Plan of action

Make the Byzantine chain components

....

Wire-wrap the tassel pearls and pearl bead links

....

Build the side chains and individual tassels

....

Complete the tassel unit

....

Connect the side chains and tassels, and add the clasp

....

Make adjustments

....

Explore & experiment

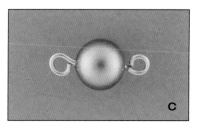

Make the Byzantine chain components

A single Byzantine segment uses 14 jump rings, and the following ones in a chain use 12 rings each. Follow the "Byzantine" weave instructions, p. 91, using 18-gauge 3.5mm rings. For the side chains, make two chains of six segments and eight chains of three segments. For the tassel chains, make one chain with seven segments, one chain with six segments, two chains with five segments, and two chains with four segments **A**.

Wire-wrap the tassel pearls and pearl bead links

String a pearl on a headpin, use roundnose pliers to make a small double loop (see "Double loops," p. 9), and trim the wire. Repeat for all six tassel-pearls: two green, two gold, and two brass **B**. My double loops used ¾ in. (1.9cm) of wire. Trim the end off a headpin. Use roundnose pliers to make a small simple loop (see "Simple loops," p. 7). String a pearl. Make another small, simple loop, and trim the wire. My simple loops used ⅝ in. (1.6cm) of wire. Repeat to make 12 pearl components: four green and eight brass **C**.

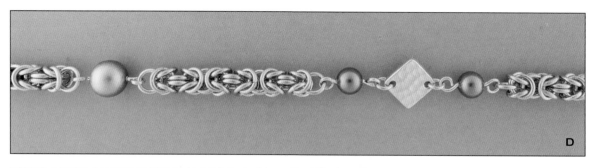

D

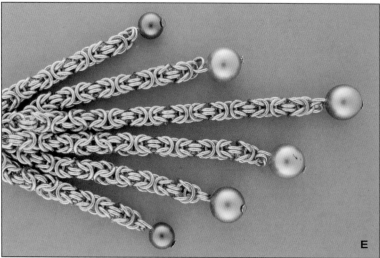

E

Build the side chains and individual tassels

Use 20-gauge 2.8mm jump rings to connect a brass pearl component to each side of all four metal links. Set out two green pearl links, two metal/pearl links, and five chain components (one of six units and four of three units). Next, you'll connect the parts, starting at the clasp end and working toward the center, front end of the chain.

Take a six-segment chain, remove an end ring, and re-open the second one. String a green pearl component, and re-close the ring.

Take a three-segment chain, remove an end ring, and re-open the other. String the previous green pearl component, and re-close the ring.

Remove a ring from the other end of this chain, and reopen the other ring. String a metal/pearl link, and re-close the ring **D**.

Continuing this pattern, add a three-unit chain, a green pearl link, a three-unit chain, a metal/pearl link, and a three-unit chain. Repeat to make a second side chain (see main project photo).

Set out the six tassel chains and the pearls for the tassels. At one end of each chain remove one ring. One-by-one, re-open the remaining ring, add a pearl bead link, and re-close the ring. Here's the plan: seven-unit chain, green pearl; six-unit chain gold pearl; five-unit

chains, one gold and one green; four-unit chains, both brass **E**.

Complete the tassel unit

Take a 4-in. (10cm) piece of wire, and make a small double loop at one end. Add five 20-gauge 2.8mm jump rings, one-in-one, to the double loop to make a mini-chain. Set out six more of these jump rings, and the six tassel chains. Use a ring to add the seven-unit tassel to link 5 (the end link) of the mini-chain. Add the six-unit tassel to link 3. Add the five-unit tassels to link 2, one to each side of the chain. Add the four-unit tassels to link 1, one to each side of the chain. Thread the wire through the bottom of the bead cap and through a green pearl. Finish the end of the wire with a wrapped loop **F, G**.

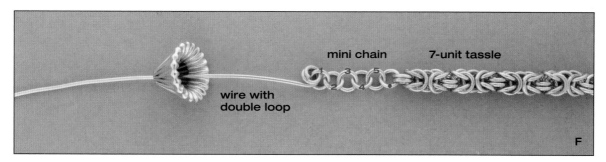

wire with double loop

mini chain   7-unit tassle

F

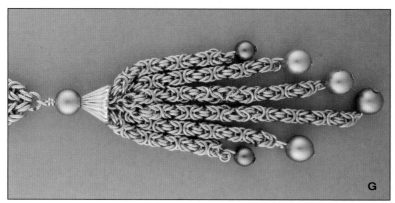

G

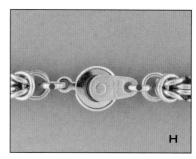

H

Connect the side chains and tassels, and add the clasp

Open two 18-gauge 3.5mm jump rings. Thread a ring through the last ring pair of the three-segment component at the end of both side chains, and also through the top loop of the tassel unit. Double up that ring (red dot) **G**.

Open two 16-gauge 3mm jump rings. Use one to add each half of the clasp at the ends of the side chains (the six-segment component) (red dots) **H**.

Make adjustments

The necklace can be made much longer by adding additional pearl links and Byzantine chain sections in pairs, one on each side, next to the clasp. The necklace can be made shorter by removing individual Byzantine segments from the six segment chains next to the clasp.

Explore &experiment

For a simple bracelet, make a single chain of Byzantine and add a clasp. Add a pearl link at the center of the chain, if you wish. For earrings, choose smaller bead cones. Wire-wrap them with three tassels, and attach to earring findings.

Oriental Drama in Black Necklace

This extraordinary glass pendant was created by a glass artist whose work has been featured in numerous gallery exhibits. I debated with myself at length to decide on the metal color, the weave, and the design to best showcase this glass piece. It looks fantastic on bare skin or a light-colored fabric.

SKILL LEVEL: Intermediate

WEAVE: Japanese 12-in-2

DIMENSIONS: 18½ in. (47cm) necklace with 4-in. (10cm) bib/pendant

MATERIALS

JUMP RINGS
- **400** 18-gauge (AWG) 5mm I.D. (large)
- **824** 20-gauge (AWG) 3mm I.D. (small)

WIRE
- 2½ in. (6.4cm) 20-gauge wire, black

BEADS
- **1** 2-in. (5cm) flower pendant (Karina Guévin, Montreal QC)

FINDINGS
- **1** 15mm lobster clasp, black

TOOLS
- **2** pairs of pliers suitable for chain mail (flatnose, chainnose, bentnose)
- Pair of roundnose pliers
- Pair of flush cutters

Note: The jump rings for this project were made from round, black enamelled copper wire (Parawire). For black or copper wire, use 3mm I.D. for the small jump rings. For Argentium sterling, 10% silver filled or Jewellers Bronze jump rings, use 2.8mm I.D. for the small rings. If you use a coated wire for this project, I recommend that you use tool dip on your pliers. For these small rings it is useful to have a pair of thin, narrow, short nose pliers like those made by Xuron.

Plan of action

- Make the Japanese flower components
- Build the side chains
- Build the center section
- Wire-wrap the pendant bead
- Connect the side chains and pendant
- Attach the clasp
- Make adjustments
- Explore & experiment

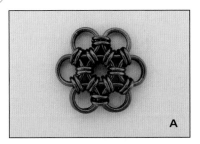

A

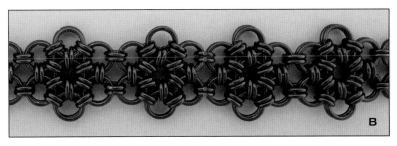

B

Make the Japanese flower components

Each Japanese Flower component uses 24 large and 24 small jump rings. Follow the "Japanese 12-in-2" weave instructions, p. 102, and repeat to make 28 flower components in total. Each component is 21mm in diameter **A**.

Build the side chains

Set out nine Japanese Flower components. Open eight pairs of four small rings. Set two components side-by-side so two petals of one flower are touching two petals of the next. Use two rings to connect both pairs of petals (red dots). Continue adding one flower at a time to make a side chain. Each flower you add will take four more small rings. Continue until all nine flowers are connected **B**. Repeat to make a second side chain.

Build the center section

Set out 10 flower components in a triangle: four, then three, then two, and one at the base to form a triangle. Open 72 small jump rings and close four large rings.

Connect the rows (12 pairs of small rings, red dots):

• Use six pairs to connect the top row of four flowers side-by-side, just as you did for the side chains.
• Use four pairs to connect the next row of three flowers.
• Use two pairs to connect the next row of two flowers.

Connect Row 1 to Row 2 (12 pairs of small rings, green dots):

• Use two pairs to connect the top of the Row 2 middle flower to the bottom corners of the two middle flowers in Row 1.
• Use one pair to connect the bottom of the second flower of Row 1 to the top corner of flower 1 in Row 2.
• Use one pair to connect the bottom of the third flower in Row 1 and the top corner of flower 3 in Row 2.

At this point, add two pairs of new large rings between Row 1 and Row 2 (pink dots). Continue:

• Use four pairs of small rings to connect a pair of new large rings at the left edge between Rows 1 and 2.
• Use one pair to connect the top of flower 1 to Row 2.
• Use one pair to connect the bottom of flower 1 to Row 1.
• Use one pair to connect the bottom corner of flower 1 to Row 1.
• Use one pair to connect the bottom corner of flower 2.
• Repeat with four pairs of small rings to add a pair of large rings at the right edge, between Rows 1 and 2.

Connect Row 2 to Row 3 (eight pairs of rings, dark blue dots):

• Use two pairs to connect the bottom of flower 2 in Row 2 to the top corners of the two flowers in Row 3.
• Use two pairs to connect the top of flower 1 in Row 3 to the bottom corners of flowers 1 and 2 in Row 2.
• Use two pairs to connect the top of flower 2 in Row 3 to the bottom corners of flowers 2 and 3 in Row 2.
• Use one pair to connect the bottom of flower 1 in row 2 to the top corner of flower 1 in Row 3.
• Use one pair to connect the bottom of flower 3 in row 2 to the top corner of flower 2 in Row 3.

Connect Row 3 to Row 4 (four pairs of small rings, light blue dots):

Rotate the Row 1 flower so there are two petals at the top.
• Use two pairs to connect the top left petal to the bottom corner and bottom petal of flower 1 in Row 2.
• Use two pairs to connect the top right petal to the bottom corner and bottom petal of flower 2 in Row 2.

note Each colored dot represents two small, connector jump rings. It is important to add the rings marked with red dots first (join each row), then the rings marked with green dots (connect the rows). It is helpful to work from the center outwards when adding a row of flowers.

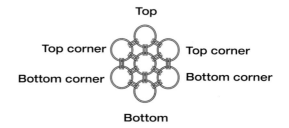

Top
Top corner   Top corner
Bottom corner   Bottom corner
Bottom

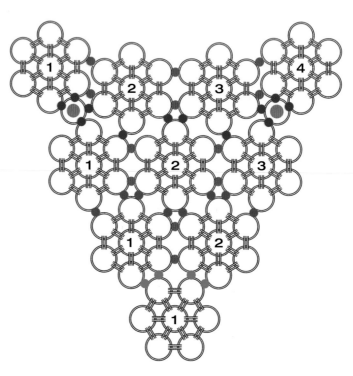

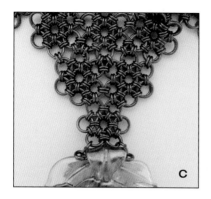

Wire-wrap the pendant bead

Make a simple loop at one end of the piece of wire (see "Simple loops," p. 7). String the pendant bead. Make another simple loop at the other end of the wire. Trim the wire as needed.

Connect the side chains and pendant

Open eight small rings. Use four small rings to connect one side chain with an end flower of the center section—just as you connected the previous components. Repeat with the other side chain and the other end flower. Open two large rings. Use the large rings to connect each loop of the wired pendant bead to a bottom petal of the flower in Row 4 (red dots) **C**.

Attach the clasp

Open eight small rings and three large rings. Add a pair of small rings to both petals at the end of both side chains. Thread a large ring through the two pairs of one side chain, add the lobster clasp, and close the ring. Thread a large ring through the two pairs at the end of the other side chain. The lobster clasp will grab this ring to close the necklace **D**.

Make adjustments

The necklace can be made longer by adding Japanese Flower components in pairs, one on each side, to the side chains. Each pair will add just over 1½ in. (3.8cm) to the length.

Explore &experiment

Building different shapes with flower components has many possibilities. Then, if you combine different colors of metal—well you could spend months playing and exploring. Start by making a bunch of flowers, and then move them around to build something pleasing. (Or you could cut out paper "flowers" and play with them to design shapes.) For a simple bracelet, make a single chain of Japanese Flowers and add a clasp. You can connect them with two connections (as you did here), or you can rotate the flowers a bit and have only one connection between flowers. For earrings, add a single flower to an earring finding, and then finish it off with a drop bead.

Beau's Bead Necklace

This exquisite lampwork bead was created by Beau Barrett. My challenge was to create a necklace that would complement its beauty. I eventually chose the Foursquare (B2G) weave, along with some Box Chain units as the back chain. My big find was some Unicorne teardrop beads in the perfect shade to echo the teal color of the focal.

SKILL LEVEL: Beginner Plus

WEAVES: Foursquare (or B2G) and Box Chain

DIMENSIONS: 16½ in. (41.9cm) necklace with a 2½-in. (6.4cm) pendant

MATERIALS
JUMP RINGS
- **732** 18-gauge (AWG) 4.5mm I.D. (small)
- **23** 18-gauge (AWG) 6.75mm I.D. (large)
- **4** 16-gauge (AWG) 3mm I.D. (for the clasp)

BEADS
- Pendant bead, art glass (Beau Barrett, Evolving Creations)

- **12** mini teardrop beads (Unicorne Beads #2341)

FINDINGS
- **1** 3-in. (7.6cm) 18-gauge headpin, sterling silver
- **1** toggle clasp, sterling silver

TOOLS
- **2** pairs of pliers suitable for chain mail (flatnose, chainnose, bentnose)
- Pair of roundnose pliers
- Pair of flush cutters

Note: The jump rings for this project were made from round, half-hard, Argentium sterling wire. These ring sizes also work for regular sterling, 10% silver-filled, jeweler's bronze, or copper jump rings. Choose your focal bead first, and then choose your accent beads to complement it.

Plan of action

Make the Foursquare components

....

Wire-wrap the pendant

....

Connect the Foursquare units

....

Connect the center Foursquare unit, pendant, and beads

....

Build the Box Chain back chains

....

Attach the clasp

....

Make adjustments

....

Explore & experiment

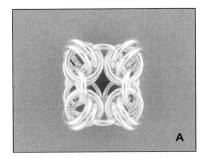

A

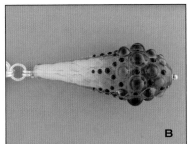

B

C

Make the Foursquare components

The correct name for this weave is B2G—but I think my name, Foursquare, is a better descriptor. The necklace is built with Foursquare segments plus a Box Chain back chain. Each Foursquare unit uses 28 small jump rings and one large jump ring. Follow the "Foursquare" weave instructions, p. 100, and repeat to make 23 components in total. Each component is about ⅝ in. (1.6cm) square **A**.

Wire-wrap the pendant

String the pendant bead on the headpin. I chose a heavy headpin with a pretty ball end to support this bead. Use roundnose pliers to

make a double loop (see "Double loops," p. 9). Trim the wire **B**.

Connect the Foursquare units

Open eight small rings. Use two rings to connect two corners of one Foursquare unit to two corners of the next (red dots). Build a chain of five units **C**.

Open three small rings (red dots). Use one ring to add just the top corners of three more Foursquare units (for a total of eight units in your chain). Open three small rings (green dots) to add a second row of three Foursquare units below the last three units you added. These rings gather up the two rings at the bottom corner of the top unit

BUILD SHAPES

71

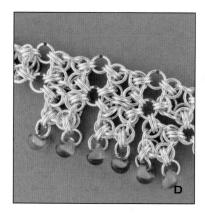

D

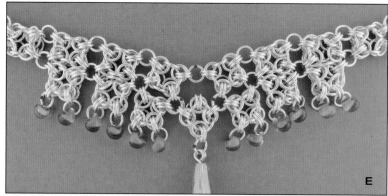

E

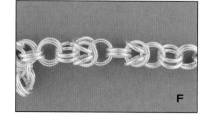

F

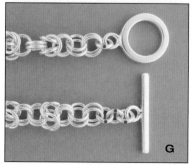

G

and the two rings at the top corner rings of the units below. The short, double row is part of the center focus of the necklace **D**. Repeat to make another chain.

Connect the center Foursquare unit, pendant, and beads

Set out the two side chains and join them together at the top corners with a small ring. Take the remaining Foursquare unit, and set it below the joining ring you just added. Turn it so it's a diamond shape. Open four small rings. Use two rings to connect a corner of the "diamond" to the bottom corner of the top row and the top corner of the second row of the side chain. Repeat on the other side. Use another small ring (red dot). to add the pendant at the base of the "diamond."

Use small rings to add the teardrop beads to the bottom corners of the second row components **E**.

Build the Box Chain back chains

Open 22 small rings. Add four pairs of rings to the top corner of the last Foursquare unit of one of the side chains. Fold the end pair of rings one to each side, and lock them in place with another pair of rings (see the "Box Chain" weave instructions, p. 90). Add three pairs of rings, fold the end pair, and lock them in place with another pair (second Box Chain unit). Add two more pairs of rings. One short back chain is now complete. Repeat to make the other back chain **F**.

Attach the clasp

At the end of one back chain, use a clasp 16-gauge 3mm jump ring to add the ring half of the toggle. At the end of the other back chain, add two more of these jump rings in a one-in-one mini-chain. Use a third ring to add the loop half of the toggle bar **G**.

Make adjustments

The necklace can be made longer by adding Box Chain components to each side of the back chain, next to the clasp. Each matching pair will add 1 in. (2.5cm) to the length. Each Box Chain unit requires eight jump rings.

Explore & experiment

For a straightforward bracelet, make a single chain of Foursquare components, and add a clasp. You can also add beads to the rings that connect one unit to the next—or you can play with different ways of joining one component to the next or combinations of metals (see "Nightscape Necklace," p. 77, as an example). For earrings, add one corner of a single unit to an earring finding (making a diamond shape). Then finish it off with a drop bead at the opposite corner.

Yin Yang Necklace

Building shapes with the Möbius weave offers unlimited design possibilities. Here, I decided to build a necklace that combines black and silver rings, and that led me to the Yin Yang Taoist concept of dark and bright—duality forming a whole.

SKILL LEVEL: Intermediate

WEAVE: Möbius

DIMENSIONS: 36 in. (.9m) necklace
with 2¾-in. (7cm) pendant

MATERIALS
JUMP RINGS
• Silver
  221 16-gauge (AWG) 5mm I.D.
  49 18-gauge (AWG) 5.25mm I.D.
  134 18-gauge (AWG) 4.25mm I.D.
  5 18-gauge (AWG) 4.5mm I.D.
• Black
  222 16-gauge (AWG) 5.25mm I.D.
  49 18-gauge (AWG) 5.5mm I.D.
  134 18-gauge (AWG) 4.5mm I.D.

CLASP
• **1** 15mm lobster clasp, black

TOOLS
• **2** pairs of pliers suitable for
  chain mail (flatnose, chainnose,
  bentnose)

*Note: The jump rings for this project
were made from round, 10% silver-
filled wire, and black enamelled copper
wire (from Parawire). These ring sizes
for silver also work for Argentium
sterling or jeweler's bronze jump rings.
Copper could be used instead of black
at the given sizes.*

Plan of
action

Make the small flower
components

. . . .

Make the large flower
components

. . . .

Make the back and
front chains

. . . .

Link everything
together

. . . .

Attach the clasp

. . . .

Make adjustments

. . . .

Explore & experiment

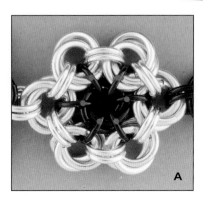

A

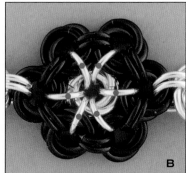

B

Make the small flower components

For the flower Möbius units, use only three jump rings for each unit (see the "Möbius" weave instructions, p. 105): 16-gauge 5mm jump rings in silver, or 16-gauge 5.25mm jump rings in black. Use 18-gauge 5.25mm rings in silver, or 18-gauge 5.5mm rings in black as connector rings.

Silver Flowers: Make five small flowers with an outer ring of Möbius units in silver, and a black Möbius in the center.
- For the outer ring, follow the "Möbius" weave instructions to make the first Möbius unit. Set it down carefully. Make the second Möbius. Link these two units with two connector rings. Continue until you have six Möbius units linked in a chain.
- Make a single Möbius unit for the

center of the flower.
- Use a connector ring to join the center Möbius to one Möbius in the chain you just made. Continue to add a connector ring from each Möbius in the chain to the Möbius in the center (green dots). When all six Möbius units are connected to the center unit, add the final two connector rings to complete the outer chain as a circle **A**.

Black Flowers: Make five more small flowers with outer Möbius units in black, and the center Möbius in silver **B**.

Make the large flower components

Large Silver Flower: Set out a small flower with a black outer ring. Using the silver rings, make a chain of 12 Möbius units. As you work, connect each Möbius to the next with two silver connector rings.

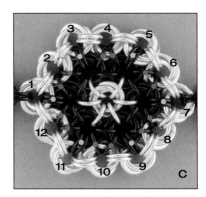

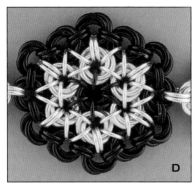

Back Chains 15 Möbius Units in Each

Small Silver G

Small Black H

Front Chain I

- Use two black connector rings (yellow dots) to link the first Möbius in the chain to one of the black Möbius units on the outer ring of the small flower. Notice that the second silver Möbius will sit in between two of the black Möbius units of the flower. Use a connector to link to each of these units. Use two more connectors (green dots) to link the third Möbius in the chain to the second black Möbius on the outer ring of the small flower. Repeat so you have a pair of black connector rings in the 1st, 3rd, 5th, 7th, 9th, and 11th black Möbius that go directly to a silver Möbius. The black connectors in the 2nd, 4th, 6th, 8th, 10th, and 12th black Möbius link to two silver Möbius units, one to each side. When all 12 Möbius units are connected to the black edge of the small flower, add the final two silver connector rings to the outer chain to complete the circle C.

Large Black Flower: Repeat the steps to make the second large flower. Start with a small flower with a silver outer ring. Use black rings to make the chain of Möbius units, and silver connector rings to finish the assembly D.

Make the back and front chains

Use silver rings to make a back chain of 15 Möbius units. Unlike the flower units, each Möbius will use four rings. Each Möbius is linked to the next with two connector rings. Repeat to make an identical back chain with black rings. Make a silver front chain of three Möbius units. Make a black front chain of three Möbius units. Use one silver and one black connector ring to connect these two short chains together E, F.

Link everything together

Set out the small flowers in black pairs and silver pairs.

Silver Flowers: Make a four-ring black Möbius, and use two pairs of black connectors to link it in between two silver flowers. Repeat with two more silver flowers G.

Black Flowers: Make a four-ring silver Möbius, and use two pairs of silver connector rings to link it in between two black flowers. Repeat with two more black flowers H.

Add the Front Chain: Use two black connector rings to link the black side of the front chain to a silver flower pair. Use two silver connector rings to link the silver side of the front chain to a black flower pair I.

Add the Large Flowers: Use two black connector rings to add the large silver-edge flower to the small black flower at one end of the front chain. Use two silver connector rings to add the large, black-edge flower to the small silver flower at the other end of the front chain J.

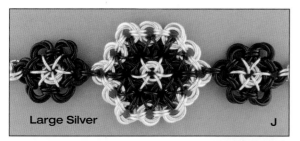

Large Silver   J

Large Black   K

Add Small Flowers: Use two black connector rings to add the large silver-edge flower to a pair of small black flowers. Use two silver connector rings to add the large black-edge flower to a pair of small silver flowers **K**.

Add the Back Chains: Use two silver connector rings to join the silver back chain to the small black flower at the end of the front section. Use two black connector rings to join the black back chain to the small silver flower at the end of the front section **L, M**.

Attach the clasp

Starting at the end of the silver back chain, add the 18-gauge 4.5mm jump rings, one into the next. Use all five rings. At the end of the black back chain, use a 16-gauge 5.25mm jump ring to connect the lobster clasp directly to the end Möbius unit **N**.

Back Chains

L

Make adjustments

The necklace can be made longer by adding additional black and silver Möbius units in pairs to the back chains, one on each side, next to the clasp. Each pair will add ¾ in. (1.9cm) to the length. You can make a longer extender chain by adding silver 18-gauge 4.5mm rings.

M

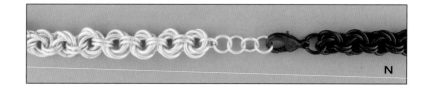

N

Explore & experiment

For a simple bracelet, make a single chain of Möbius units and add a clasp. Or, link several small flowers together, with or without a Möbius in between each one. Another option is a large flower as a focal, with a small one on each side—joined with a series of Möbius units.

For earrings, a small flower added to an earring finding would be dramatic. You could make a silver edge one for one ear, and a black edge one for the other. Or, for long, dangly earrings, create a chain of three to five Möbius units—silver for one ear, and black for the other.

Nightscape Necklace

I'm very intrigued with the design possibilities of the B2G weave—which I've re-named Foursquare. In this necklace, I played with silver and black squares because I wanted to feature a stunning Navette faceted crystal pendant bead from Swarovski.

BUILD SHAPES

SKILL LEVEL: Beginner Plus

WEAVES: Foursquare (B2G) and Barrel

DIMENSIONS: 20½ in. (52.1cm) necklace with 2¾-in. (7cm) pendant

MATERIALS

JUMP RINGS
- Silver
  20 18-gauge (AWG) 3mm I.D.
  98 18-gauge (AWG) 3.5mm I.D.
  216 18-gauge (AWG) 4.5mm I.D.
  18 18-gauge (AWG) 6.75mm I.D.
  16-gauge (AWG) 8mm I.D. (for pendant)
- Black
  64 18-gauge (AWG) 3.5mm I.D.
  112 18-gauge (AWG) 4.5mm I.D.

BEADS
- 1 40x18 Navette pendant, jet (Swarovski)

CLASP
- 1 6mm magnetic button clasp, silver

TOOLS
- 2 pairs of pliers suitable for chain mail (flatnose, chainnose, bentnose)

Note: The jump rings for this project were made from round wire. These ring sizes will work for Argentium sterling, 10% silver filled, copper, or jeweler's bronze jump rings. The jump rings could be any one metal, or any two metal combination.

Plan of action

Make the Barrel Weave back chains

⋯⋯⋯⋯⋯⋯⋯⋯

Make the Foursquare components

⋯⋯⋯⋯⋯⋯⋯⋯

Connect the Foursquare and Barrel components, and the pendant

⋯⋯⋯⋯⋯⋯⋯⋯

Attach the clasp

⋯⋯⋯⋯⋯⋯⋯⋯

Add the pendant

⋯⋯⋯⋯⋯⋯⋯⋯

Make adjustments

⋯⋯⋯⋯⋯⋯⋯⋯

Explore & experiment

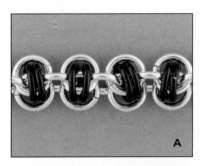

A

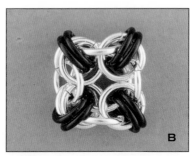

B

C

D

Make the Barrel weave back chains

Follow the "Barrel Weave" instructions, p. 89, to make two chains, each with 16 barrels. Use 18-gauge 3.5mm jump rings in silver and black. In the first step, the three open rings are silver, and the two closed rings are black. Each component uses these five rings **A**.

Make the Foursquare components

Follow the "Foursquare" weave instructions, p. 100, to make 18 components. Use small 18-gauge 4.5mm jump rings in silver and black, and large 6.75mm jump rings in silver. In the first step, the eight open rings are silver, and the eight closed rings are black. In the last step, the large ring will pick up the pair of black rings from each of the four units. Each component uses 12 silver 4.5mm rings, eight black 4.5mm rings, and one silver 6.75mm ring **B**.

Connect the Foursquare and Barrel components, and the pendant

Make the side chains: Open seven silver 3mm rings. Set out seven

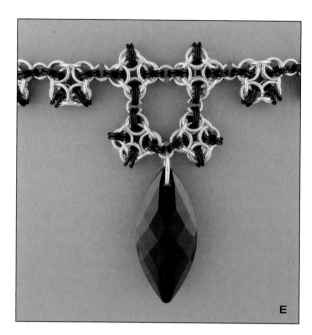

E

F

Foursquare components and one Barrel back chain. Hold an open ring in your pliers, and pick up two black corner rings from one Foursquare component and two black corner rings from another. Close the ring (green dots). Use the remaining small silver rings to connect the seven components in a chain **C**.

Use the seventh silver ring to connect this side chain to a Barrel back chain (green dot) **D**. Repeat this step to join another set of seven Foursquare components together and connect them to the other Barrel back chain.

Build the front section: Open four silver 3mm rings. Set out the four remaining Foursquare components. As you did before, join the set of four components into a chain. Then, very carefully, arrange them into a diamond shape, and add the final connecting ring. Open two silver 3mm rings. Turn the top left square so it's a diamond shape. Connect the end black rings of a side chain to the top, left corner of the diamond shape. Repeat to add the other side chain to the Front section. Use the 16-gauge 8mm jump ring to connect the pendant to the connector ring at the base of

the front section **E**. See the green dots for connection points.

Attach the clasp

Re-open the end ring of a back chain, and add the loop of half of the clasp. Re-close that ring. Repeat to add the other half of the clasp to the other back chain **F**.

Make adjustments

The necklace can be made longer by adding additional pairs of Barrel units, one on each side, next to the clasp. Each pair will add ½ in. (1.3cm) to the length. Each Barrel requires five additional rings: three silver and two black.

Explore & experiment

For a simple bracelet, make a single chain of barrels and add a clasp. Or make a chain of Foursquare units, but connect both the top and bottom of each square to the next. For earrings, add one corner of a Foursquare unit to the earring finding, and attach a small jet drop at the bottom corner. Or, make a short chain of three to five barrels, and add a drop bead.

Art Deco Necklace

Before I started working with chain mail, I spent several years doing beadwork. This special pendant is one of mine. It has multiple layers of square stitch using Delica beads, and is trimmed with Swarovski crystals. I decided to use chain mail to build a chain for it. I chose gold-filled and black rings with blue zircon bicone crystals to reflect the beadwork colors and embellishments.

SKILL LEVEL: Beginner

WEAVE: Byzantine

DIMENSIONS: 22 in. (56cm) necklace with 3¾-in. (9.5cm) pendant

MATERIALS
JUMP RINGS
- **514** 18-gauge (AWG) 3.5mm I.D., gold-filled
- **306** 18-gauge (AWG) 3.5mm I.D., black

BEADS
- **16** 6mm bicone crystals, blue zircon (Swarovski)

FINDINGS
- **2** 3-to-1 strand connectors, gold color
- **16** 2-in. (5cm) headpins, black
- **1** 9x15mm snap clasp, gold

TOOLS
- **2** pairs of pliers suitable for chain mail (flatnose, chainnose, bentnose)
- Pair of roundnose pliers
- Pair of flush cutters

Note: The jump rings for this project were made from round, gold-filled wire, and black enamelled copper wire from Parawire. These ring sizes also work for Argentium sterling, 10% silver-filled, jeweler's bronze, or copper jump rings. I recommend choosing your pendant first, and then choosing accent beads in appropriate colors.

Plan of action

Make the Byzantine chain components
....
Wire-wrap the bead components
....
Connect the chains and bead links, and add the pendant
....
Attach the clasp, connectors, beads, and chains
....
Make adjustments
....
Explore & experiment

gold and black   gold   black

A

Make the Byzantine chain components

Follow the "Byzantine" weave instructions, p. 91, using 18-gauge 3.5mm jump rings. Make two gold and black chains: Start with five gold Byzantine units, but when you get to the last unit, switch to black for the two locking rings. Continue the chain with three more black Byzantine units.

Make one chain with six gold Byzantine units. Make two chains, each with five gold Byzantine units. Make five chains, each with three gold Byzantine units. Make six chains, each with three black Byzantine units **A**.

Wire-wrap the bead components

Use the black headpins to make 14 wire-wrapped crystals (just clip off the ends): Make a simple loop (see "Simple loops," p. 7), string a crystal, and then finish with another simple loop. The loops should be fairly small, but large enough to accommodate two 3.5mm jump rings **B**.

Use two headpins (with the ends on) to make two bead dangles: String a crystal on a headpin, and finish with a wrapped loop (see "Wrapped loops," p. 8) **C**.

Connect the chains and bead links, and add the pendant

Inner Chain: Set out two gold and black chains, three three-unit gold chains, two three-unit black chains, and six wire-wrapped crystals. Start with a gold/black chain, add a bead link by opening one of the loops (use two pairs of pliers and open it as you would a jump ring), add the pair of rings at the end of

B

C

D

E

F

G

H

the chain, and close the loop. See the photo to add the remaining components **D**.

Outer Chain: Set out the six-unit gold chain, two five-unit gold chains, two three-unit gold chains, and four three-unit black chains. Start with a five-unit gold chain. Refer to photo **E** to add the remaining components.

The Pendant: Push the end of the outer chain through the bail of the pendant. Carefully slide the pendant along to the center of the chain **F**.

Attach the clasp, connectors, beads, and chains

Open two gold rings. Pass the open ring through the loop of one half of the snap clasp and through the single loop side of the connector, and then close the ring. Repeat to add the other connector to the other half of the snap clasp. Open two black rings. Thread an open ring through the loop of a wire-wrapped crystal and through the middle loop of the connector. Repeat with the other crystal (red dots) **G**.

Open four gold rings. Use two gold rings to connect the end pairs of

the outer chain to the outside loops of the connector. (This is the chain with the pendant.) Repeat for the inner chain (red dots) **H**.

Make adjustments

The necklace can be made longer by adding additional Byzantine units, four at a time, one at both ends of both chains, next to the connector. Or, add a single strand of Byzantine units as back chains. Add it between the connector and the clasp, on both sides of the necklace. A Byzantine unit measures ½ in. (1.3cm). One complete unit requires 14 rings, but an added-on unit uses 12 rings.

Explore & experiment

Explore the possibilities of combining the two colors of rings and the bead links to make a multi-strand bracelet and coordinating pair of earrings. Use headpins to make bead drops for the earrings—just don't cut the ends off! Simply add the crystal to a headpin, make a simple loop, and you're done.

Beneath The Sea Necklace

Several years ago I purchased a bracelet from Muriel Duval, a Montreal glass bead artist. It was a delightful combination of her beads and stick pearls. I wore it a few times but was always thinking about how I could take it apart and then re-combine the pieces with chain mail. This necklace is the result.

Make Byzantine components

Follow the "Byzantine," weave instructions, p. 91, using 18-gauge 3.5mm jump rings. Make two back chains, each with eight Byzantine units. Make 16 single Byzantine units **A, B**. Make one chain with 4½ Byzantine units. Make one chain with 6½ Byzantine units.

Make European 4-in-1 components

Follow the "European 4-in-1," weave instructions, p. 98, using 18-gauge 3.5mm jump rings. Make three lengths of chain, each with 12 repeats. Each repeat uses seven rings. You can tell the number of repeats by counting rings along the outside edge **C**.

Wire-wrap the stick pearls

You will need a bit less than 3½ in. (8.9cm) of 20-gauge wire to wrap each stick pearl. Make a wrapped loop (see "Wrapped loops," p. 8), and string one hole of a stick pearl. Finish with another wrapped loop. Repeat for the other hole **D**. The loops should be fairly small, but large enough to accommodate a 3.5mm ring. Repeat for the other stick pearl.

A

B

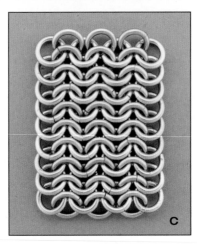

C

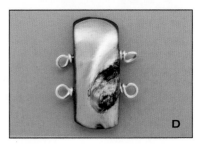

D

Connect the chain components and beads

Set out the two back chains and four single Byzantine units. Open eight jump rings. Use one ring each to join two Byzantine units to the end of both back chains. For each chain, use two rings, side-by-side, to connect together the end pairs of rings of the two Byzantine units, right at the join (see **I**, red dots).

Set out a back chain, the two smaller art glass beads, six single Byzantine units, and two European 4-in-1 chains. Open 14 jump rings. Use two rings to connect each of the Byzantine units at the end of a back chain to the European 4-in-1 chain. Thread a ring through the end pair of the Byzantine unit, and the second ring in from the edge of the Euro unit. Use two rings to link the bottom edge (second ring in) of the Euro unit to each of two more Byzantine units. Use two rings to link those Byzantine units to two loops of a glass bead. Continue to use pairs of rings to add two Byzantine units, one European 4-in-1

E

F

G

H

unit, two Byzantine units, and one smaller glass bead **E–H**.

Set out a back chain, the larger art glass bead, two stick pearls, six single Byzantine units, and a European 4-in-1 unit. Open 14 jump rings. Repeat the strategy for the first side. Use pairs of jump rings to connect components in this order: one stick pearl, two Byzantine units, one large glass bead, two Byzantine units, one European 4-in-1 unit, two Byzantine units, and one stick pearl **I, J**.

Add the two center chains: Open four jump rings. Take the longer center chain and connect one end to the outer loop of the stick pearl, and the other end to the outer loop of the art glass bead. Repeat to add the shorter center chain to the inner loops of the stick pearl and the glass bead.

Attach the clasp

Open four jump rings. Use one ring to connect the ring part of the toggle clasp to one of the back chains. Add two rings, one-by-one, to the end of the other back chain. Use one ring to connect that last ring to the bar part of the clasp **J**.

Make adjustments

Your beads are unlikely to be exactly the same as mine, but the layout can be similar. Start by setting out the back chains and the front chains. Next, set out your beads and the larger European 4-in-1 sections. You may have to make the Euro sections longer or shorter, but first add the Byzantine units and center chains to the beads. The goal is to make the two sides approximately the same length. Have fun playing.

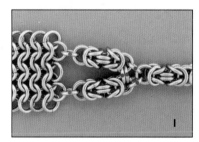

I

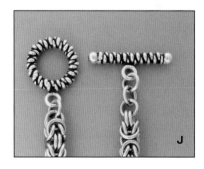

J

Explore & experiment

Use an art glass bead as the focal point of a bracelet. Add two Byzantine chains to each side, or use European 4-in-1 chain to construct the sides.

Maple Leaf Forever Necklace

I love this creative, fold-formed pendant by Marilyn O'Connor, and when I examined the leaf, I was sold. It closely resembles a maple leaf, the national symbol of Canada—and 2017 is Canada's 150th birthday. I used copper and silver jump rings to reflect the metals in the pendant, and settled on rectangular segments of the Byzantine Filigree pattern to complete a winning combination.

SKILL LEVEL: Intermediate

WEAVES: Byzantine, Byzantine Filigree

DIMENSIONS: 23½ in. (59.7cm) necklace with a 1-in. (2.5cm) pendant

MATERIALS

JUMP RINGS
- **100** 18-gauge (AWG) 6.5mm I.D., Argentium sterling (large)
- **280** 18-gauge (AWG) 3.5mm I.D., Argentium sterling (small)
- **340** 18-gauge (AWG) 3.5mm I.D., copper (small)
- **8** 18-gauge (AWG) 3mm I.D., Argentium sterling

PENDANT
- **1** 1x1¼-in. (2.5x3.2cm) pendant (Marilyn O'Connor, Tucson AZ)

FINDINGS
- **2** glue-on bails, rhodium
- **1** toggle clasp, sterling silver

OTHER SUPPLIES
- Tube of E-6000 glue or 2-part epoxy glue

TOOLS
- **2** pairs of pliers suitable for chain mail (flatnose, chainnose, bentnose)
- Awl

Note: The jump rings for this project were made from round, Argentium sterling silver wire and round, fully hardened copper wire. These ring sizes also work for silver-filled and jeweler's bronze jump rings.

Plan of action

Glue the bails to the pendant

Build the Byzantine filigree chain of component

Add the Byzantine back chain

Attach the pendant

Attach the clasp

Make adjustments

Explore & experiment

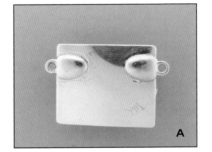

A

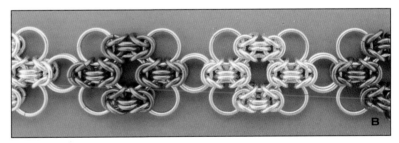

B

Glue the bails to the pendant

This step is first so the glue will dry thoroughly. The bails are glued to the side edges of the pendant, and the top edge of each bail is about 3mm down from the top edge of the pendant **A**. (Note: I chose a pendant without a bail as part of the structure. I wanted to play with the positioning and not be limited by a single bail).

Build the Byzantine filigree chain

Follow the "Byzantine Filigree" weave instructions, p. 92, using large silver 18-gauge 6.5mm jump rings and small copper 18-gauge

3.5mm rings. Then, switch to the small silver rings, return to the first step, and add two small silver rings to the last large silver ring added. Repeat all the steps once again. Continue to alternate colors until you have a chain that is seven components in length **B**. Four units will use small copper rings, and three will use small silver rings. Repeat to make another chain for the other side of the necklace.

Add the Byzantine back chain

Next, add a short, three-segmant, Byzantine chain to one end of each side chain. Follow the "Byzantine" weave instructions, p. 91, using

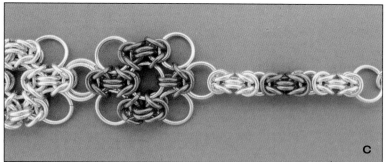

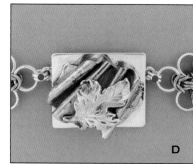

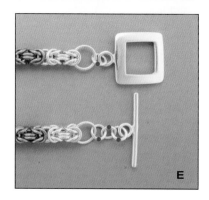

12 small silver 18-gauge 3.5mm rings. In the first step, add two small rings to the large silver ring at one end of the Byzantine Filigree chain you just completed. For the next Byzantine segment, use 10 small copper rings. Use two silver rings for the final "locking" step. For the third Byzantine segment, use small silver rings. When you reach the last step, use a large silver ring as the "locking" ring **C**. Repeat to add a three-segment Byzantine chain to the other side chain.

Attach the pendant

Use four 3mm silver rings as connector rings. Use two rings to connect a bail on the pendant to the large, silver ring of the end Byzantine Filigree components of each side chain (red dots) **D**.

Attach the clasp

Use four 3mm silver rings for the connectors. Use a ring to connect the loop half of the toggle to the large silver ring at the end of the back chain (red dot). Starting at the large silver ring at the end of the other back chain, use three rings to make a mini one-in-one chain (red dots). Connect the bar half of the toggle to the last ring **E**.

Make adjustments

The necklace can be made longer by adding additional Byzantine segment in pairs, one on each side, next to the clasp. Alternate the metal used for the segments—the next unit would be copper. Each pair will add 1 in. (2.5cm) to the length. Each component requires 12 additional jump rings.

Explore & experiment

For a bracelet, make a single chain of Byzantine Filigree components, and add a clasp. A smaller, complementary version of the foldform pendant could be the focal point of a bracelet.

Appendix of Weaves

Barrel

This weave is attributed to Susan Richards and is on the mailleartisans.com website.

SKILL LEVEL: Beginner
PROJECT: Nightscape Necklace, p. 77
ASPECT RATIO: 3.4–3.5

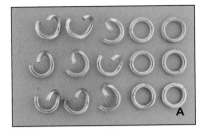

Make sets of three

Prepare several rows of five rings, each with three open and two closed **A**. Hold one open ring with the pliers, add two closed rings, and close the ring (red dot) **B**. Repeat to prepare more sets of three rings. Each set of three will use two more rings to connect it to make the barrel chain.

Make the first segment

Pick up another open ring (red dot) and insert it through the single ring of a set of three rings and through a large paperclip or twist tie. Close the ring **C**. You now have a short chain of one ring—one ring—two rings attached to a handle.

Take an open ring (red dot), place it through the end pair, and hold it there with your pliers **D**.

Use your other hand to lift the chain upward, with the first ring tipped away from you (very important) **E**.

Moving from front to back, hook the ring you're holding through the first ring **F**. Close the ring.

Make the second segment

Insert an open ring (red dot) through the sides of the two horizontal rings of the previous segment, and then through the single ring of a set of three rings (blue dot) **G**. Close the ring **H**.

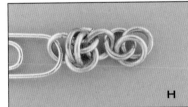

Insert an open ring through the end pair of rings and then front to back through the first ring of the segment (red dot) as you did before **I**, **J**.

Repeat these steps to make additional Barrels. Finish the chain with a single ring through the sides of the last pair of horizontal rings. It will match the very first ring in the chain **K**.

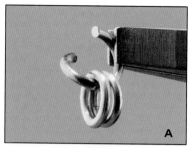

A

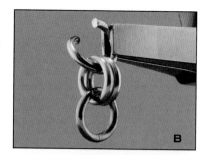

B

C

D

E

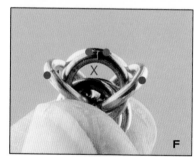

F

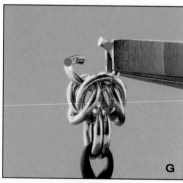

G

H

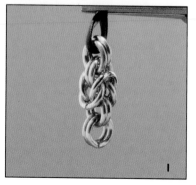

I

J

Box Chain

This pattern is composed of short, repeating segments. Each complete segment after the first has six jump rings: two shared rings and four new rings.

SKILL LEVEL: Beginner
PROJECT: Beau's Bead Necklace, p. 70
ASPECT RATIO: 3.9–4.4

Getting started

Close two rings and open two rings. Hold one open ring with the pliers, gather up the two closed rings **A**, and then close that ring.

Add the other open ring along the same path **B**. Attach a twist tie or piece of wire to an end pair of rings so you have a "handle" to hold **C**.

The pattern

Add a pair: Open two rings. Insert these rings one by one (red dots) into the end pair (blue dots) **D**.

Flip and fold: Hold the twist tie so the last two pairs of rings are above your thumb and first finger. Flip the end rings (red dots), one to each side **E**. Fold those two rings down, and then turn everything around so you can hold the folded rings between your fingers.

Separate and lift: Separate the two middle rings (red dots). Peek between them and see the top edges of the two end rings you folded to the sides (red dots). You can use an awl, a piece of wire, or something similar to help lift up those two center rings. The next two rings will pass through the rings with the red dots, and the blue X marks the space to insert the next ring **F**.

Lock: Open two rings. Pick up an open ring with your pliers (green dot) and insert it through this path. Close the ring **G**. Add a second ring through this same space, and close it (green dot). This is one complete segment **H**.

Repeat

Repeat "The pattern" until the chain is the required length. **I** shows the first pair of rings added at the end—all ready to fold, separate, and then lock in place. **J** shows two completed Box Chain segments.

Byzantine

The Byzantine chain mail pattern is composed of segments that are linked together by a shared pair of jump rings at each end. Each complete segment uses 14 jump rings. In a continuous chain, the two end rings of one segment are shared by the next, so the following segments each use only 12 rings each.

SKILL LEVEL: Beginner
PROJECTS: Smoky Bronze Links Necklace, p. 16, Byzantine Windows Necklace, p. 42, Trizantine Necklace, p. 50, Byzantine Star Pendant, p. 53, Byzantine Circle Pendant, p. 56, Princess Tassel, p. 59, Tassels and Pearls Necklace, p. 62, Beneath the Sea Necklace, p. 83, and Art Deco Necklace, p. 80
ASPECT RATIO: 3.4–3.9

Getting started

Start by following "Getting started" and "The pattern" of "Box Chain," p. 89. This forms the first half of a Byzantine segment **A**.

The pattern

Add two pairs of rings: Open six rings. Insert two rings (one by one) (blue dots) into the last pair (green dots). Insert another pair of rings into that pair (red dots). You now have three linked pairs of rings hanging down **B**.

Fold, separate, and lock: Fold the end pair of rings. Separate the top pair. Insert two locking rings (review "Box Chain" as needed) **C**.

Byzantine segment

Repeat: To make a continuous Byzantine chain, keep repeating "The pattern" (add two pairs, fold, separate, and lock). Refer to "Box Chain" as needed **D**.

A

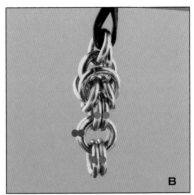
B

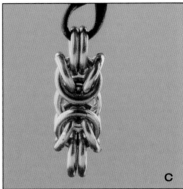
C

D

Byzantine Filigree

This weave has three rows of Byzantine segments arranged in an offset pattern. The segments are connected on the top, bottom, and sides with larger rings, giving it a lovely filigree appearance.

SKILL LEVEL: Intermediate
PROJECT: Maple Leaf Forever Necklace, p. 86
ASPECT RATIOS: 6.4 and 3.4 (two sizes)

Make the starter unit

The starter unit is a Byzantine segment that is surrounded on all sides by large rings. This sets the width of the chain.

Open 10 small rings and two large rings. Close one large ring. Add two small rings to the large closed one (red dots) **A**.

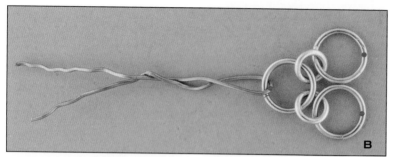

Add a wire handle to the large ring. Add a large ring to each small ring (red dots) **B**.

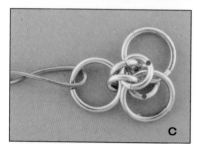

Add a small ring through the pair of small rings. Turn your work over, and add a small ring through the same rings (red dots) **C**.

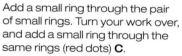
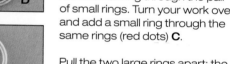
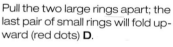

Pull the two large rings apart; the last pair of small rings will fold upward (red dots) **D**.

Add two small rings through the bottom edges of the rings that folded up (do not go through the large ring) (red dots) **E**.

Add two small rings through the previous pair (red dots) **F**.

Place a small ring through a large side ring and the last pair of rings. Repeat for the other large ring (red dots) **G**.

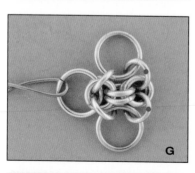

Add a large ring to lock in the first Byzantine segment. This can be tricky—use an awl or piece of wire to help you open up the space where the large ring will go. If you have trouble, unfold the pair of small rings, and refold them with the awl ready to be inserted **H, I, J**.

Make a Byzantine segment on each side

Add two small rings: one to connect two large rings (a side and a center one), and the second to a large side ring (red dots) **K**.

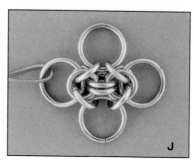

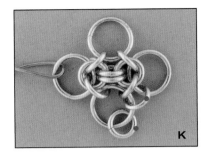

K

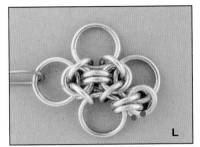

L

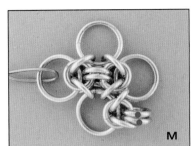

M

Add one small ring through the last pair. Turn the work over, and add another to the same pair (red dots) **L**.

Fold the second pair up. The next pair of rings go through the bottom edges of the folded rings (red dots) **M**.

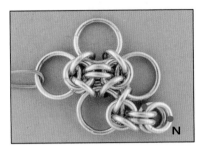

N

O

Add another pair of rings to the previous pair (red dots) **N**.

Add another pair of rings to the previous pair, with one ring also going through the large center rings (red dots) **O**.

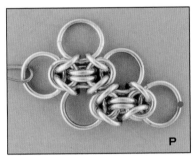

P

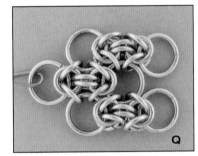

Q

Lock in the fold with a large ring (red dot) **P**.

Repeat "Make a Byzantine segment on each side" to make a matching Byzantine segment on the other side **Q**.

Make a Byzantine segment in the middle

Add two small rings. Each one goes through the center ring and one of the side rings (red dots) **R**.

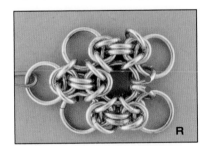

R

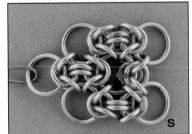

S

Add one small ring through the last pair. Turn the chain over and add one more to the same pair (red dots) **S**.

Fold the last pair up. Place two small rings through the bottom edges of the rings that were folded up (red dots) **T**.

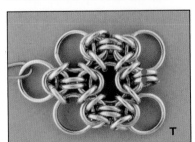

T

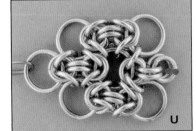

U

Add another pair of rings to the previous pair (red dots) **U**.

Add another pair of rings to the previous pair. Both rings will also go through the large side rings (red dots) **V**.

V

W

Lock in the fold with a large ring (red dot) **W**. This is a single component. Repeat to make another component. Repeat the last two sections to make a continuous chain.

A

B

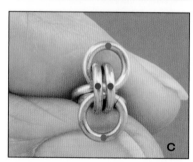

C

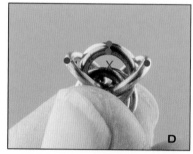

D

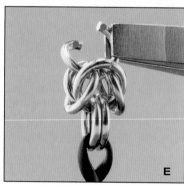

E

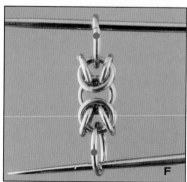

F

Byzee Beez to Butterflies

The Byzee Beez to Butterflies weave has segments of 10 rings that are joined side-to-side with one ring across the top half and another across the bottom half.

SKILL LEVEL: Intermediate
PROJECT: Beez Beads Necklace, p. 44
ASPECT RATIO: 3.9

Getting started
Close six rings and open four rings. With your pliers holding an open ring (blue dot), add four closed rings (red dots); close that ring. Pick up another open ring (blue dot) and go through the same four closed rings; close that ring. Arrange the rings as in the photo **A**.

Pick up another open ring, pass through two end rings, and add two closed rings (red dots); close that ring (blue dot). Pick up another open ring, and go through the same four closed rings; close that ring (blue dot). Arrange the rings as in the photo. You will have five pairs of rings linked together. Repeat to make additional mini-chains (each Beez Bead requires six) **B**.

Add temporary rings
Open several large temporary rings (you will use them to hold the rings in each segment as a traditional Byzantine segment). They will help keep the rings under control at the beginning while you link the sides of the segments. These rings are also useful as "handles."

Fold the rings: Hold a mini-chain so the end two pairs of rings are above your thumb and first finger. Flip the end rings (red), one to each side. Now fold those two rings down and hold the folded rings between your thumb and first finger **C**. The middle rings (blue) will be at the top.

Separate the two middle rings (red dots). Peek between them and see the top edges of the two end rings you flipped to the sides (blue dots) **D**. If needed, you can use a toothpick, a piece of wire, or something similar to help lift up those two center rings. The blue X marks the space to insert the next ring!

Lock in the fold temporarily: Pick up an open temporary ring with your pliers and insert it through the space marked with the blue "X" in the previous photo (green dot). Close the ring **E**. Turn to the other end of the segment, and follow the previous two steps to place the second temporary locking ring.

This photo shows the temporary rings in place (green dots) **F**. Prepare six segments with temporary rings so they are ready to connect side by side.

Connect the segments side by side

Set two segments beside each other with the edge of the temporary rings sitting so the front of each component is facing you. The red dots show where to place the first connecting ring. You will be passing a ring through the sides of the folded-down rings of each segment. Imagine an open ring going through the left segment, then curling around and coming back up through the right segment **G**.

First segment: Make sure the large, temporary ring is on edge toward you as in the previous photo. Pick up an open ring (red dot), and go front to back through the sides of the two rings that were folded down—these are the two rings that the temporary ring is holding **H**.

Second segment: Now, pick up the second segment and go through the two side rings on it by curling the ring around from the back to the front (red dot) **I**.

The second connector: Turn the pair of segments upside down. Insert the second connecting ring just as you did in the first segment (red dot) **J**.

Continue to make a short chain by adding the remaining four segments, one at a time, next to the pair you just finished **K**. Remove and re-use the large temporary rings as necessary.

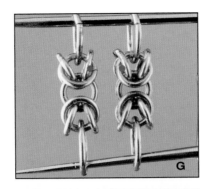

G

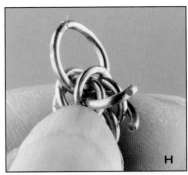

H

I

J

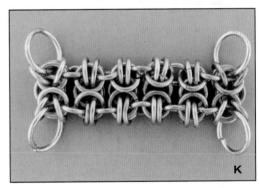

K

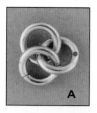

A

B

Chinese Knot

The original name of this chain mail pattern is Pheasible, but to me, the weave looks like Chinese knots. It is composed of segments that are linked together by one ring. Each complete segment uses 10 rings. One more ring joins two segments together.

SKILL LEVEL: Beginner Plus
PROJECT: Ode to Bisbee Necklace, p. 26
ASPECT RATIO: 2.9–3.2

Create a Chinese Knot component

Open eight rings and close two rings. Hold an open ring with the pliers and add on the two closed rings. Close that ring (red dot) **A**.

Pick up an open ring and put it through the same two closed rings

C

D

E

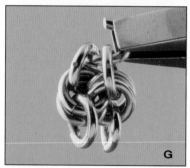

G

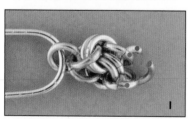

I

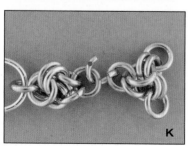

K

(red dot)—now you have a chain of two pairs of rings **B**.

Add two rings (one by one) to the end pair of the chain (red dots)—now you have a chain consisting of three pairs of rings **C**.

Add two more rings to the end pair of the chain (red dots)—now you have a chain of four pairs of rings **D**.

The red arrows show the easiest way to pick up the next two rings (green dots). You may find it helpful to lay the chain of linked rings on your index finger and hold it with your thumb as you use the pliers to pick up a ring from each end **E**.

Hold an open ring with the pliers and slip on one ring from one end pair (green dots) **F**.

Then add a second ring (red dot) from the other end pair (green dots). **G**.

Note: If you set your work down, notice there are three rings sticking out to choose from. Two of them go through a parallel pair of rings. The third one goes through a pair of rings that are on an angle (because you picked them up from opposite ends of the beginning mini-chain).

Immediately connect this ring (red dot) to a paper clip or wire so the next two rings you'll connect (green dots) can be easily identified **H**.

Hold an open ring with the pliers (red dot), and slide on these two rings (green dots). Close the ring **I, J**.

Repeat the previous steps to make the next segment. Before you set down your pliers, use another ring to connect that last ring to the end ring of the previous segment (red dot) **K**.

Now add the final ring to complete this second segment (red dot) **L**.

F

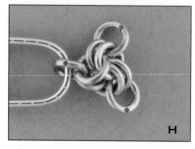

H

J

L

Chrysanthemum

The Chrysanthemum weave is a variation of the Circular European 4-in-1 weave.

SKILL LEVEL: Beginner Plus
PROJECT: Chrysanthemum Links Necklace, p. 20
ASPECT RATIOS: 5.9, 4.9, and 2.9 (three sizes)

Getting started

Make the flower center: Open two large rings for the center of the flower. Close eight small rings. Open eight small rings **A**.

Hold an open large ring in your pliers and pick up the eight closed small rings. Close the ring **B**.

Hold another large ring in your pliers, and pass through the same eight closed rings. Be careful not to pass through the first large ring and get them crossed (red dots). Close the ring **C**.

One by one, add the remaining eight small rings through the large center rings **D**.

Add the flower petals

Open 16 medium rings for the outer row of petals **E**.

Insert an open medium ring through two of the small rings (red dots). Close the ring **F**.

Insert the next open ring in front of the previous medium ring, going in a clockwise direction. Pick up the second of the two small rings just used, plus the next free one (red dots). Close the ring **G**. Repeat, continuing to add medium rings around the center, in a clockwise direction.

Continue until you have two open medium rings left. At this point, it will get difficult to insert the open rings. Pull hard with your pliers on the one remaining small ring to get it in position and have enough space to add the second last ring (red dot) **H**.

See how the small rings are now all sitting side by side. The final ring will sit in front of the last medium ring, and behind the first medium ring (red dots) **I**.

Hold the open ring in your pliers, and pick up the first small ring used plus the second of the small rings you just placed (red dots). This will be the most difficult ring to insert—but it can be done. Fold the medium rings forward or backward to help open up the necessary space **J, K**.

Repeat all the steps to make additional Chrysanthemum components.

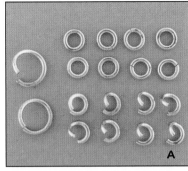

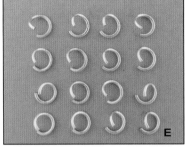

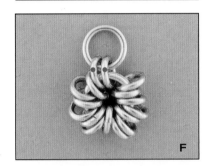

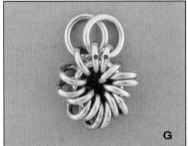

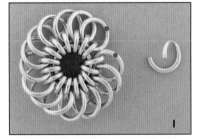

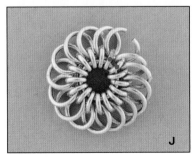

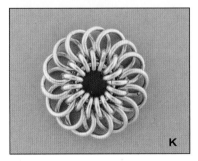

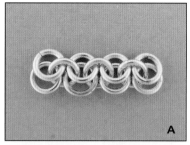

European 4-in-1

Flat mesh is another name for the European 4-in-1 weave. This weave has four rings linked to each ring and it allows you to build shapes by increasing and decreasing at the edges. It drapes and curves very much like a flexible fabric; the rings are like scales that expand and contract as they move.

SKILL LEVEL: Beginner
PROJECTS: Butterfly Wings Neck Chain, p. 10, Trizantine Necklace, p. 50, and Beneath the Sea Necklace, p. 83
ASPECT RATIO: 3.1–3.4

Getting started

The starting row for a rectangle will begin and end with a pair of rings, and each pair is linked to a single ring. This example of a rectangle has four pairs of rings, and it takes three rings to join the pairs together. Adapt the instructions to create a wider or narrower piece of chain.

Close eight rings, and open three rings. Hold an open ring with your pliers and gather up four closed rings. Close that ring. Hold an open ring with your pliers, gather up two closed rings at the end of your chain, and add two closed rings. Hold the open ring with your pliers, gather up two closed rings at the end of your chain, add two closed rings, and then close that ring. Arrange your work to look like the photo **A**. Play with the rings to lay them out neatly. Try rolling them around between your thumb and index finger until they lay flat. Then set them down on your work surface and rotate them as needed. The length of the foundation row sets the width of the chain.

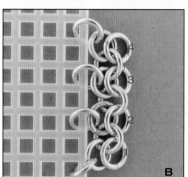

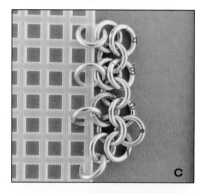

Set out a piece of plastic canvas (see p. 5) and your starter chain. Open four rings. Use the open rings to connect one ring of each pair of your chain to the canvas (I skipped one hole between each ring) **B**.

Make a rectangle shape

Row 1: Open three rings. Notice the four numbered edge rings. You are going to link them together. Hold an open ring in your pliers. Pass down through ring 1 and up through ring 2. Close the ring (red dot) **C**. Join rings 2 and 3, and 3 and 4 the same way (red dots) **D**.

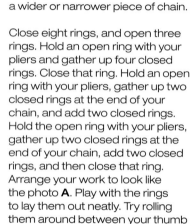

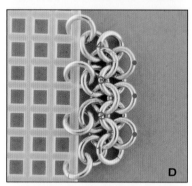

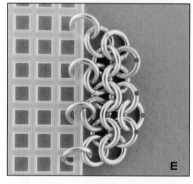

Row 2: Open four rings. Use two of the rings to link together the four rings from Row 1. This photo shows the first ring (green dot) in place **E**. Add the second ring (green dot) **F**.

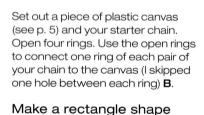

Add a ring at each side (green dots). Each end ring only goes through one ring—it hangs loose, but it will get connected in the next row **G**. Row 2 is now complete.

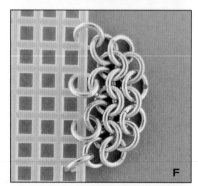

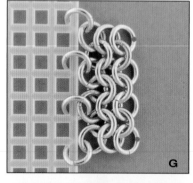

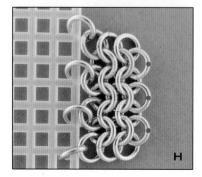

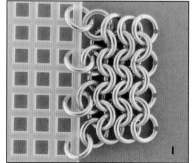

Repeat Row 1, adding three rings (red dots) **H**.

Repeat Row 2, adding four rings (green dots) **I**. Continue to repeat these two rows for the length of your rectangle.

Join two ends of a rectangle

The edges to be joined must both end in the same number of rings. In this example, both ends have four rings: two outside edge rings and two interior rings. If adding a row to one edge, this row would have three rings. So, to join these two pieces you need three rings. Add two rings to start, one at each side of your work. Each of these rings passes down through two rings (one on each edge), and then curls around and up two more rings (one on each edge). The goal is to have the connecting rings lay in the same orientation as the rest of the rings in that column **J**.

The third ring is easier to add because the sides are stabilized. This ring also picks up two rings from one edge and two rings from the other edge **K**.

Build a butterfly wing

Close two rings and open one ring. Add the closed rings to the open one, and close the ring. Arrange the rings so the single ring is at the bottom **L**. Add a piece of wire or a twist tie to this single ring.

Open a stash of rings. Insert a ring through the pair of rings in the previous row (red dot) **M**.

Insert a ring through the first and the last rings of the previous row (red dots) **N**. (These are the rings that expand the width of the shape.)

Starting at one side, insert a ring through each overlapping pair of rings in the previous row (red dots) **O**. Insert a ring through the first and the last rings of the previous row (red dots) **P**. Repeat to add the next row **Q**.

Continue adding rows as needed. I've added three more rows so there are eight rings in the top row **R**.

Open a large ring, gather up the top row of rings, and close the ring **S**.

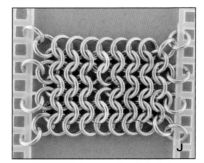
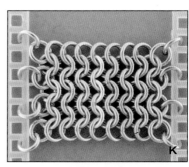

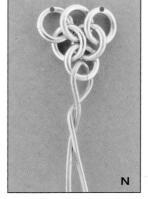
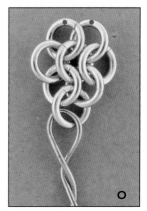
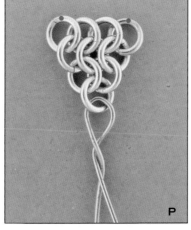
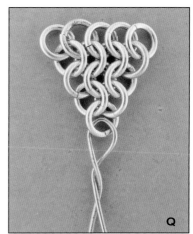
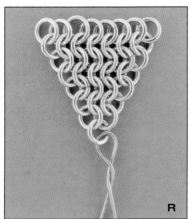

4-in-2

The 4-In-2 chain mail weave has a pair of rings placed through each previous pair. If you look in the middle of the chain, you will notice that every pair has four rings linked to it—hence, the name.

SKILL LEVEL: Beginner
PROJECTS: Lusty Links Neck Chain, p. 13, and Byzantine Star Pendant, p. 53
ASPECT RATIOS: 3.9 and 2.9–3.4 (two sizes)

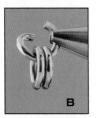

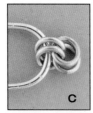

Getting started

Close two rings and open additional rings, setting them out in pairs **A**.

Hold an open ring in your pliers and add the two closed rings **B**. Close the ring.

Add a second ring beside the single ring at the end of the chain. Add a piece of scrap wire or a paperclip to the pair of rings to give you a handle **C**.

Pattern repeat

Add two rings (one by one) to the end pair of rings **D**. Repeat until your chain is the desired length **E**.

Shortcut Note: To begin, you can open half the rings and close half the rings. Later, instead of adding all the rings one by one, you can start each new pair by adding two closed rings as in the second step.

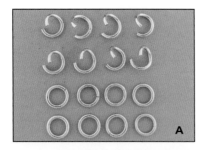

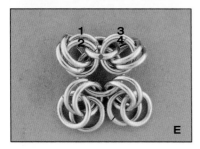

Foursquare (B2G)

This weave is on the mailleartisans.org website and is named B2G. I decided that Foursquare was a more descriptive name.

SKILL LEVEL: Beginner Plus
PROJECTS: Beau's Bead Necklace, p. 70, and Nightscape Necklace, p. 77
ASPECT RATIOS: 4.4 and 6.6 (two sizes)

Make 2-in-2 units

Open eight small rings and close eight small rings **A**.

Hold an open ring in your pliers, add two small closed rings, and then close that ring. Add a second ring through the same two closed

rings. You have two rings linked to two rings **B**. Make three more 2-in-2 units.

Add four units to a center ring

Open 12 small rings and one large ring. Hold the large ring (red dot) in your pliers, and pick up an end pair of each of the four units. Close the ring **C**.

Connect the four units to make a square

Fold down the end pair of rings of one unit—one ring to each side. Hold them folded while you fold down the rings of the next unit **D**. The sides of the four rings that are touching are marked with red dots.

Hold an open ring in your pliers and pick up the two side rings of these two units—the four rings that touch each other. Close the ring (red dot) **E**. This requires some dexterity, but once you get the first one done, the others are easier.

Continue to connect one folded-down set to the next until all four units are connected to their neighbors (red dots) **F**.

Repeat steps 1–7 to make more Foursquare units. See the specific project instructions for details on how to connect them together.

Inverted Roundmaille

This chain mail weave is some- times called open round chain mail, and it is related to the European 4-In-1 weave. The chain is solid and round, yet open and airy—well suited for bracelets and necklaces.

SKILL LEVEL: Beginner
PROJECT: Oriental Beads Necklace, p. 47
ASPECT RATIO: 3.9–4.0

Easy start

Row 1:
Open three rings. Place the rings at a corner of a piece of plastic canvas (see p. 5) so they form a triangle **A**. In this example, I placed the smaller rings (20-gauge 3.25mm) in the top corner, and the larger rings (18-gauge 4mm) at the bottom corner. The rings are set in a triangle because this weave is a round, hollow tube.

Row 2: Open three rings, and link the previous three rings as shown in the photo **B**. Open up rings and lay them out in sets of three. This way, you won't get confused about whether or not you've completed a row.

Row 3: Open three rings, and link the previous three rings as shown in the photo **C**. Notice that I've taken the photo upside down—this is so the last row of rings will dangle down. Otherwise, they fold down over the previous row, and it's hard to tell which rings to connect.

Keep adding three rings to each row. As you work on the chain, hold the most recent row snugly between your thumb and first two fingers so the edges of the last three rings are touching **D**.

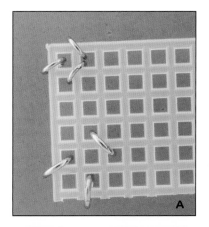

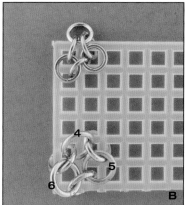

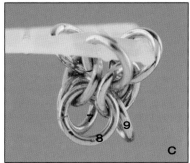

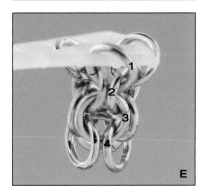

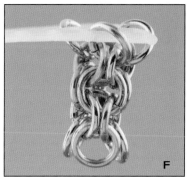

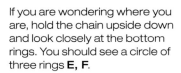

If you are wondering where you are, hold the chain upside down and look closely at the bottom rings. You should see a circle of three rings **E, F**.

Japanese 12-in-2

The Japanese 12-in-2 weave is composed of small rings and large rings, all in pairs. The small rings sit upright, and the large rings lay flat. The center of each "flower" is a large ring pair surrounded by six "petals." Wherever the large rings touch each other, they are connected by pairs of small rings.

SKILL LEVEL: Beginner
PROJECT: Oriental Drama in Black Necklace, p. 66
ASPECT RATIOS: 4.9 and 3.5 (two sizes)

Make a center circle of rings

Open two large rings (not too wide). Close 12 small rings. Hold an open ring in your pliers, gather up the 12 small closed rings, and close the ring. There's not a lot of room for the pliers, so chainnose pliers or bentnose pliers are helpful **A**.

Hold the second large ring in your pliers and feed it through all 12 small rings. It will sit as a second layer on top of the first large ring. Be careful not to cross the other large ring. Close the ring. This is the center of the flower **B**.

Add a top layer of large rings

Open six large rings. Insert a large ring through two small ones in the flower center. Insert another large ring through the next two small rings **C**. Repeat until there are six large rings surrounding the center ring and all 12 small rings are in place **D**.

Connect the large rings

Open 12 small rings. Link each pair of large ring petals with two small rings **E, F**.

Double up the large rings

Open six large rings (not too wide). Insert one large ring on top of each large ring around the center of the flower **G**. Maneuver each ring carefully so you pass through all six small rings. Be careful not to cross the two large rings **H**.

Repeat to make additional Japanese Flower components.

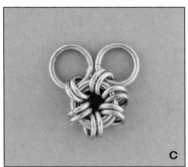

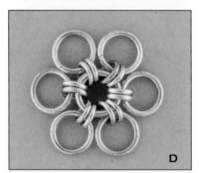

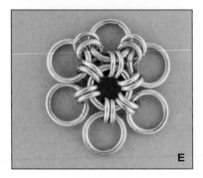

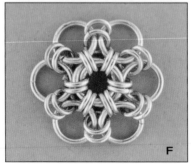

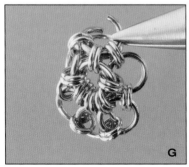

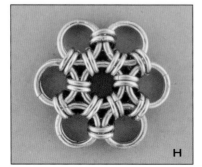

Japanese Ball

This weave requires 84 rings to make one ball. Choosing rings to make this ball is very important. If the ring is slightly too small, it will be impossible to finish stitching the halves together. If the ring is slightly too large, the ball will be a bit floppy (you can stuff the inside with something: beads, or even closed rings). If you make the two halves of a ball, and you find it too tight to finish joining together, you can use the halves as bead caps!

SKILL LEVEL: Intermediate
PROJECT: Oriental Beads Necklace, p. 47
ASPECT RATIO: 4.2–4.3

Getting started

The Japanese Ball is made in two halves that are then joined together. Close 12 rings and open 20 rings to make the first half of the ball. Use six closed rings and four open rings to make a chain that is five pairs long (see "4-in-2," p. 100) **A**.

The middle pair of this chain will become the center of this hemisphere (red dots). Use two closed rings and two open rings to add two pairs to the center **B**.

Use two closed rings and two open rings to add another "arm" to the center **C**. Use two closed rings and two open rings to add the fifth arm to the center **D**. Use two open rings to start connecting the ends of the "arms" (red dots). Go up one pair and down the next with your rings **E**.

Use eight open rings to continue connecting the arms into a circle. When you add the last pair, you will notice that the circle starts to become concave **F**.

Repeat to make a second hemisphere. To help keep oriented as you join the halves, add a piece of wire or a twist tie under the pairs of rings that are the arms of the "master half" (believe me, it can get confusing if you don't!) **G**.

Open 20 rings. Now, you'll start to stitch the halves to make a ball. Choose one arm of the master half, and use two open rings (red dot) to connect with one arm of the other half, and two more rings (red dot) to connect to an adjacent arm. Notice

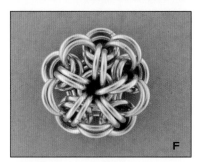

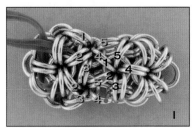

the end of this master half arm now holds five pairs of rings (green numbers) **H**. Each arm on the master half connects to two arms of the second half.

Move to the next arm of the master half. Add two rings (red dot) to connect it to an arm connected in the previous step. Notice that there are now five pairs (black numbers) of rings at the end of that arm on the other half. Add two more rings (red dot) to a new arm of the other half. Notice that the end of this master half arm now holds five pairs of

rings (more green numbers) **I**. As you add these pairs, be careful so no rings are crossed—it's very difficult or impossible to fix later. Keep repeating the last step as you work your way around the master half **J**. You must be methodical—you can't just connect arms here and there!

As you add the final few rings, the opening is small. It helps if you insert the ring from under, going upwards. Then grab the other end of the ring and go under and up to connect the second pair of rings.

Jens Pind

SKILL LEVEL: Intermediate
PROJECT: Byzantine Circle Pendant
ASPECT RATIO: 2.9–3.1

Make a three-ring mobius
Rings 1 and 2: Connect two rings together. Hold ring 2 (that you just closed) in your right pliers **A**.

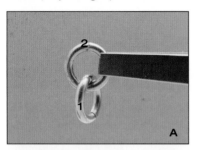

With your left hand, swing the dangling ring over to the right, and lower ring 2. Notice that it sits in front of ring 1 **B**.

Ring 3: Keep holding those two rings in your left hand. Pick up an open ring with your pliers, and insert it through those two rings, front to back. With both pliers, close the ring **C**.

Set down your left pliers. With your left hand, swing the dangling rings over to the right, and lower ring 3 in front of the previous rings **D**.

Make the Jens Pind chain
Hold the Möbius between your index finger and thumb. Notice the top halves of the rings are coming toward you—this is a left-handed Möbius. The red dot marks the spot where you will insert the next ring. It goes through the top two rings on the right **E**.

Insert and close this ring. Next, use your right pliers to lay the rings between the index finger and thumb of your left hand, moving the previous two rings over to the right **F**.

The red dot marks the spot where you will insert the next ring. It goes through the top two rings and to the right of the third ring. Use your left thumb on ring 3 to help open up this space **G**.

Repeat "Make the Jens Pind chain" until you have the desired length of chain. Stop from time to time to slowly rotate the chain and make sure each line of rings down the length of the ring are like stair steps. Also, notice how one row of rings (red lines) slants upward, and the row of rings beside it (black lines) slants slants downward, forming "V" shapes **H**.

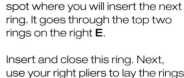
Extra Help

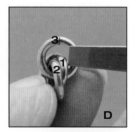

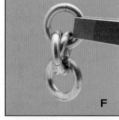
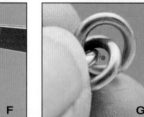

What if I have to set my work down? Try to set it down with the front facing up. When you pick it up again, insert the next ring. Before you close it, look at the back side of the ring to be sure it is following the "step" pattern. If it isn't, flip the chain around and insert the ring from the other side. Then continue onward.

What if I don't know which end I was working on? It doesn't matter which end you work from.

Möbius Ball

This Möbius ball (or flower, or nest) is composed of two or more rings. Each ring added to the ball passes through all of the previous rings. These instructions are for a right-leaning Möbius, where each new ring stacks behind the previous one. In a left-leaning Möbius, each new ring stacks in front of the previous one.

SKILL LEVEL: Beginner
PROJECTS: Mobius Drop Earrings and Yin Yang Necklace
ASPECT RATIOS: 3.9 and 4.1 (16-gauge) or 5.9 and 6.1 (18-gauge) (two sizes)

The pattern
Close one large ring and open five large rings. Open four small rings. Use pliers to insert a large ring through the closed large ring **A**, and close it.

Set down the pliers in your non-dominant hand, and use your fingers to turn the dangling ring to your left. Use the pliers, and still holding the newly closed ring, slide it sideways, behind the previous ring **B**. Keep holding the rings.

Insert a large ring (front to back)

 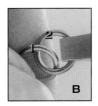  
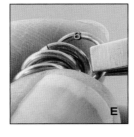  

through the center of the previous rings **C**.

Close the ring. Turn the dangling rings to the left, and then slide the new ring sideways so the top of the new ring lies behind the previous ring **D**. Keep holding the rings.

Repeat "The pattern" until you have the required number of rings nestled together. Don't change the order of the rings. Keep holding as you add the rings **E**.

Next, pick up a small ring, insert it through the center of the Möbius

ball, and close it. This locks the Möbius rings in place **F**.

For some projects, you will add two or three small rings through the Möbius **G**. For other projects, you will link two Möbius balls with one or two larger rings that pass through the center of one ball and around through the center of the second one.

Note: If you drop a Möbius ball while you are making it, it is difficult to return the rings to their original order. It's easier to just take it apart and start over.

Love Knot

The Love Knot (Fourever Chain) is an interlocking set of four pairs of jump rings. Think of it as a "doubled up" or "kinged" Möbius Ball with four rings. This is a very useful component!

SKILL LEVEL: Beginner
PROJECT: Love Knot Sparkle Necklace, p. 23
ASPECT RATIO: 4.3

Getting started
Open six rings and close two rings **A**.

Create the knots
Hold an open ring in your pliers, add the two closed rings, and close the ring. Add another ring through the same two closed rings. Close the ring **B**. Arrange the two pairs of rings so you can see the hole in the center red dot).

Use your pliers to insert a ring through this hole, and close the ring. Use your pliers to insert a sec-

  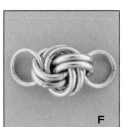

ond ring through the same hole **C**, and close the ring **D**. Arrange the three pairs of rings so you can see the hole in the center (red dot).

Use your pliers to insert a ring through this hole, and close the ring. Use your pliers to insert a second ring through the same hole, and close the ring **E**.

Repeat to create as many knots as desired.

Link the Knots
Insert a ring through a pair of rings on one side of the knot. Then, insert another ring through a pair of rings on the opposite side of the knot **F**.

APPENDIX OF WEAVES

105

Orchid

SKILL LEVEL: Beginner
PROJECT: Orchid Zipper Pull, p. 40
ASPECT RATIO: 4.3–4.4

Getting started

Close two rings (2 and 3). Open one ring, and add it to the two closed rings. Slide the single ring onto a paper clip (or attach a twist tie or a piece of scrap wire to this single ring) **A**.

The pattern

Open two rings (4 and 5). Hold the chain by the handle and let it dangle. Add one ring to each of the bottom two rings. These two new rings will be the petals that stick out on each side of the chain **B**.

Open two rings (6 and 7). The next pair of rings are added one by one, but both will ONLY pass through rings 2 and 3. Hold the chain by the handle, and focus on finding rings

2 and 3. Insert ring 6 through these two rings, and close it. Notice the two petals (4 and 5) stick out to the sides—and ring 6 is in front of them **C**.

Turn the chain completely around so ring 6 is at the back, facing away from you. Insert an open ring through rings 2 and 3 so it is in front of the two side rings. Think of it like a sandwich—these last two rings enclose the two side rings or petals of the orchid **D**.

Open two rings (8 and 9). The last pair of rings are added one by one, but both rings ONLY go through the last rings (6 and 7) you just added. This pair of rings locks in place the petal rings that stick out to the sides **E, F**.

Repeat "The pattern" to make additional orchids **G**.

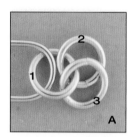

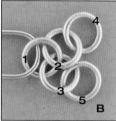

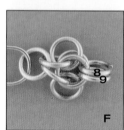

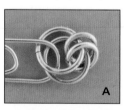

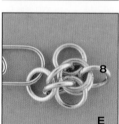

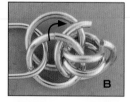

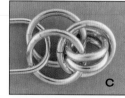

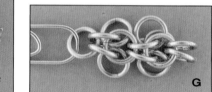

Parallel (Helm)

SKILL LEVEL: Beginner
PROJECTS: Parallel Purple Necklace, p. 30, and Parallel Zipper Pull, p. 41
ASPECT RATIOS: 5.4–6.2 and 3.3–4.3 (two sizes)

Getting started

Close two large rings and add them to a paper clip or scrap wire.

The pattern

Open two small rings. Hold an open small ring in your pliers, pass it through the two large closed rings, and close it. Pass the second small ring through the same large rings, and close it **A**.

Open one large ring. Hold the ring in your pliers, slide it between the two large rings, and surround the two small rings **B**. Close the ring **C**.

Open two large rings. Insert one large ring through the two small rings only. This ring will sit on one side of the single large ring from the previous step **D**.

Turn the chain over and insert a large ring through the same two small rings, but on the other side. This is a complete pattern **E**.

Repeat "The pattern" until your chain is the desired length. To count the number of repeats you've made, just count the number of pairs of small rings in your length of chain **F**.

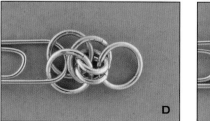

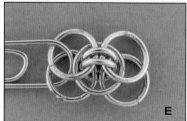

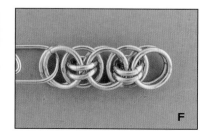

Persian GSG

The GSG chain mail pattern is a repeating set of two pairs of jump rings.

SKILL LEVEL: Beginner Plus
ASPECT RATIO: 4.9

Getting started

Cut a piece of plastic canvas (see p. 5 more details), and mark one side as the "front" or "top." I've used a marker here, but a piece of tape would work well too. Add two rings to two adjacent holes along one edge **A**.

Move the rings so they are leaning downward. Ring 1 is sitting on top of ring 2. Add ring 3 through the eye of rings 1 and 2 (an eye is the opening created where two rings overlap each other) **B**.

Hold the jump rings with ring 3 pushed up/over to the left, out of the way. The red dots mark the spots for ring 4 **C**. Insert ring 4 around the eye—go down through the centre of one ring and back up through the center of the other. Close the ring.

This photo shows ring 4 in place **D**.

Next repeat

Keep the front of the chain facing you as you work (as shown in the first step). Insert ring 5 through the eye of the last two jump rings (blue dot). Push ring 5 up/over to the left, out of the way **E**. (The red dots mark the spot for ring 6.)

Insert ring 6 around the eye of rings 3 and 4. Pass down through the center of ring 3, and back up through the center of ring 4. Close the ring **F**.

Look at the last pair of rings and notice that the top/left one sticks up higher than the one below it. This is a visual cue if you get mixed up between the front and back, and indicates which side to push the next ring to.

Following repeat

Keep the front of the chain facing you as you work. Insert the next ring through the eye of the last two jump rings. Close the ring. Push that ring up/over to the left, out of the way **G**.

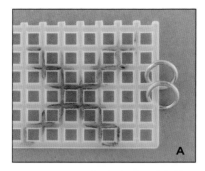

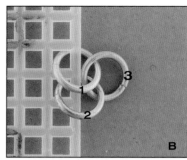

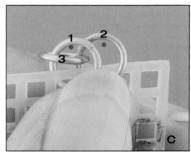

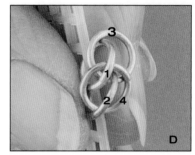

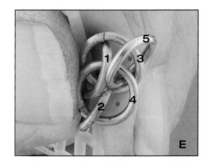

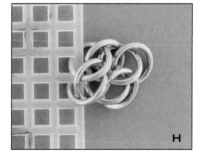

Insert the next ring around the eye of the previous pair of rings—pass down through the center of one ring and back up through the center of the other. Close the ring **H**.

Repeat "Following repeat" for the length of the chain. Remember to work on the front side, and if there's a lumpy section, you've likely made a front/back error. Always work from the previous pair of jump rings. One pair will lay flat, and the next pair will stick up a bit—but you can ignore that.

Trizantine

SKILL LEVEL: Intermediate
PROJECT: Trizantine Necklace, p. 50
ASPECT RATIO: 4.4–4.7

First half-segment

Open five rings and close three rings. Use pliers to insert three open rings through the three closed ones, one by one. Close each rings as it is connected **A**.

Looking at one set of three rings, add the two outer ones to a paper clip **B**. It's helpful to use an awl or piece of wire to separate out those two rings and grab them with the paper clip.

Add two open rings, one on each side, to the three rings at the end. Close the rings **C**.

Fold one ring down towards the paper clip on one side, and the other ring down on the other side **D**.

Turn the chain so the side is visible **E**.

Open two rings. Insert them in the spaces between the three rings (red dots). Each ring you insert will catch three rings (the two folded rings and the center ring). This is one half of a Trizantine segment **F**.

Note: The first complete segment uses 18 rings, but subsequent segments only use 16 rings each; two rings at the end of each segment are shared.

Second half-segment

Close one ring and open five rings. Hold an open ring in your pliers, pass through one ring (red dot), add a closed ring (green dot), and then pass through the other ring added in the previous step (red dot). Close the ring (blue dot). Both photos show the same step—the chain is just turned 90 degrees **G, H**.

Add two more rings through the same path (blue dots) **I**.

Turn the chain, and add two open rings through the end three rings, one on each side **J**.

Turn the chain. Fold those rings down, one to each side **K**.

Open two rings. Insert them in the spaces between the three rings **L**. This is one complete Trizantine segment using four closed rings and 14 open rings.

Repeat

To make the next half-segment, continue from "Second half-segment" and then repeat again to finish a complete segment **M**. To add a whole segment, you will use two closed rings and 14 open rings.

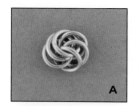
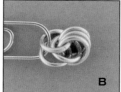
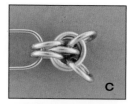
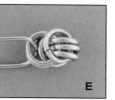
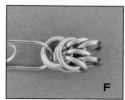
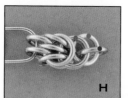

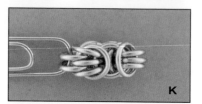

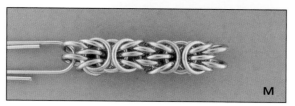

Sweetpea

This weave was named by Dylon Whyte and is a variant of the Persian family of weaves.

SKILL LEVEL: Beginner Plus
PROJECT: Sweet Chrysacolla Necklace, p. 33
ASPECT RATIO: 3.9–4.1

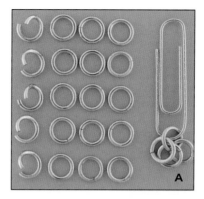

Make the starting chain
Set out rows of three closed rings and one open ring. Hold one open ring in your pliers, add the three closed rings and a paperclip, and close that ring **A**.

Hold another open ring in your pliers, grab the middle closed ring of the last three closed rings, add three closed rings, and close that ring **B**.

Repeat until you have a chain the length you need. This photo shows five units **C**.

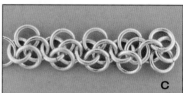

Add the locking rings
Open more rings and set them out in pairs **D**. These are the locking rings that will be added to each unit. Each locking ring is going to pass through the floppy pair and the single following ring. A locking ring will be added to both sides of every unit.

Hold an open ring in your pliers, pass through the pair of floppy rings (red dots), then curl around to pass through the next ring (blue dot), and close the ring **E**.

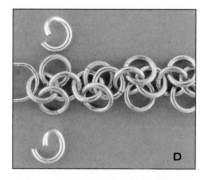

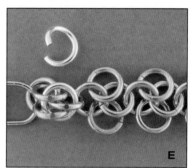

Turn the unit to the other side and repeat with the second locking ring. Hold an open ring in your pliers, pass through the pair of floppy rings (red dots), then curl around to pass through the next ring (blue dot), and close the ring **F, G**. The second locking ring is a bit trickier, and you may have to reposition your pliers to close the ring.

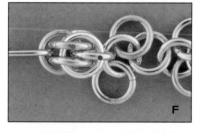

Continue to add a pair of locking rings to each of the floppy pairs. Before you add the last locking rings, add one ring to the middle ring of the three loose end rings as a handle (you can remove it later) **H**.

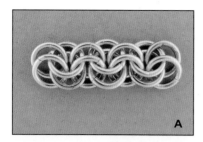

A

B

C

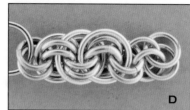

D

E

F

G

Viper Basket

SKILL LEVEL: Beginner
PROJECT: Viper Basket Earrings
ASPECT RATIOS: 4.3 and 6.8 (two sizes)

Getting started

Start by following the steps for "4-in-2" weave, p. 100. Make a chain that has seven pairs of small rings **A**. Add a paper clip (or earring wire) to the end pair of rings to give you a handle for the next steps.

Add the large rings

Open seven large rings. Hold an open large ring in your pliers. Insert it up through the first pair of small rings (the ones that are connected to the paper clip or earring wire), and then curl it around and go down through the third pair of rings. Close the ring **B**.

Take another large ring and insert it, front to back, through the second pair of small rings, and back to front, through the fourth pair of small rings. Close the ring **C**. Notice that it sits in front of the previous large ring.

Repeat, making sure you work from the same side of the bracelet **D**. Notice the stacking order: Each new, large ring sits in front of the previous large ring.

The dark pieces of wire in this photo show the path for the next ring **E**. Repeat again, making sure you work from the same side of the chain **F**.

Repeat again—you will use five of the large rings in total **G**.

Acknowledgments

Thanks to: Erica Barse, Senior Editor at Kalmbach Books, for her guidance and patience with my questions.

Anne Munro, for proofreading the weave tutorials.

My many students and customers, who have tested my instructions in classes and in their homes. I value their feedback and suggestions for improvement.

Everyone who purchased my first book, enjoyed the projects, and encouraged me to write one more.

My husband Brad, the resident Ring Master and kit assembler. Once again, I just couldn't have completed this project without his encouragement, love, and support. You can view the result of his labors at marilyngardiner.com/store.

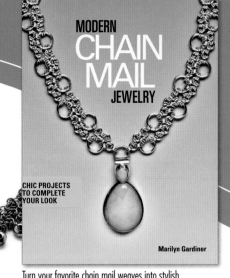
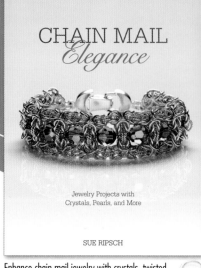

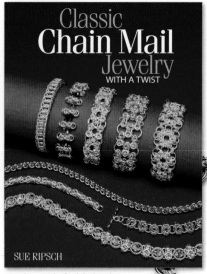